EXPLORING THE ROOTS OF SOCIAL THEORY AND INQUIRY

MAKING SENSE OF SOCIAL LIFE

First Edition

BY DEVEREAUX KENNEDY

cognella® | ACADEMIC PUBLISHING

Bassim Hamadeh, CEO and Publisher
Kassie Graves, Director of Acquisitions and Sales
Jamie Giganti, Senior Managing Editor
Jess Estrella, Senior Graphic Designer
Jim Brace-Thompson, Senior Specialist Acquisitions Editor
Brian Fahey, Senior Licensing Specialist
Bryan Mok, Interior Designer

Cover image: Copyright © Depositphotos/Rawpixel.

Printed in the United States of America

ISBN: 978-1-5165-1646-9 (pbk) / 978-1-5165-1647-6 (br) / 978-1-5165-4634-3 (al)

To Cortney Barone all by herself!

ACKNOWLEDGMENTS

The inspiration for much of what follows comes from Richard Swedberg and his colleagues' suggestion that we move from an emphasis on abstract theory per se toward an emphasis on theorizing, and from John Levi Martin's call for a reemphasis on theory work. Accordingly, this book is an attempt to help students learn how to critically examine and evaluate proposed explanations of social life and how to begin the process of constructing such explanations themselves.

The first people to be acknowledged and thanked are the students who have taken my classes, particularly my theory classes, over the years. Those students in my contemporary sociological theory course and used earlier versions of this text deserve particular mention. Their comments and criticisms have made this a much better book.

I want to express my sincere appreciation to Michaelyn Mankel, who carefully read, reviewed, and commented on the first manuscript version of this book. She did a wonderful job. Ms. Mankel is one of the best students I have ever had the privilege to teach and work with. I look forward to seeing her develop and grow both as a student and a person.

I want to thank my good friend Gavin Kitching for his close and patient reading of this book. His comments, thoughts, criticisms, and suggestions on this project, as on so many other things, have been invaluable to me.

Jim Brace-Thompson and the staff at Cognella have been extremely helpful in transforming this manuscript into a textbook. I thank them for all their good work.

Finally, I want to thank Grand Valley State University for granting me the sabbatical leave on which much of this book was written.

The book's shortcomings are on me.

TABLE OF CONTENTS

FOREWORD

SUGGESTIONS TO INSTRUCTORS ON HOW THEY MIGHT USE THIS BOOK

Exploring the Roots of Social Theory and Inquiry is an attempt to introduce students to theory in a way they can understand; demonstrate its relevance to the concerns of students majoring in a social science; and more closely connect courses in theory to introductory methodology and topic courses in social science. I hope this book makes a contribution to the contemporary movement from theory to theorizing initiated by Richard Swedberg (Swedberg 2014, Swedberg, Editor. 2014) and his colleagues.

Students are often resistant to theory. They find it intimidating, abstract, and removed from their "real" interests. I begin by attempting to overcome this resistance. I argue that the authors of social studies and students interested in social science usually start at the same place: they are curious about social life and want to sate that curiosity; they are concerned about social problems and want to address them; they are passionate against social injustices and want to redress them.

I try to show how the authors of social studies use theorizing to connect their curiosities, concerns, and passions to particular topics; and use their sociological imagination to transform topics of social relevance into social and intellectual problems. They attempt to address these problems by using theoretical concepts, data, and research methods to establish a pattern of connections between social phenomena. I suggest to students that they look at this pattern of connections as a kind of picture of social life. In effect, the authors of social studies argue that the problem they address exists because the social world looks and works the way they say it does in the picture they have created. Solving the problem they address requires a transformation of the way social life currently looks and works into something that looks and works differently. The creation of these pictures is a form of theorizing.

I have selected four social studies as examples of such theorizing: *Coming Apart: The State of White America, 1960–2010* by Charles Murray (2012); *The New Jim Crow: Mass Incarceration in the Age of Colorblindness* by Michelle Alexander (2012); *The XX Factor: How the Rise of Working Women Has Created a Far Less Equal World* by Alison Wolf (2013); and *Indigenous Methodologies: Characteristics, Conversations, and Contexts* by Margaret Kovach (2009). I use these works because they are accessible and on topics of general interest covered from widely different perspectives.

In my examination of these studies, I identify the curiosities, concerns, and passions that motivate each author. I demonstrate how the authors use their curiosities, concerns, and passions to transform topics of social interest into social or intellectual problems. I describe how each employs theoretical concepts, data, and methods to construct pictures of social life which, the author of the study argues, explain why the problem addressed exists. I describe their suggestions as to how social life would have to be changed for that problem to be solved. Finally, I evaluate each author's theorizing.

I hope that instructors use *Exploring the Roots of Social Theory* to help their students uncover, describe, and evaluate the theorizing contained in studies that their students find interesting and relevant. I also hope that *Exploring the Roots of Social Theory* will aid students in the process of learning to use their sociological imagination along with a growing mastery of concepts, data, and methods to theorize on their own. In addition to review questions, I have formulated suggested assignments and additional readings at the end of each chapter to provide students with a step-by-step guide to uncovering, describing, and evaluating the theorizing of others and to begin to do their own theorizing. Instructors using this text may well want to develop their own assignments. Whether they ask students to follow my suggestions for additional works they might read is of course up to the instructor and dependent upon the level at which the course is taught, and the instructor's view of what students in their courses can handle and benefit from.

I hope that instructors who use *Exploring the Roots of Social Theory* will employ the detailed analysis of the particular social studies analyzed in it as openings for further examination and discussion of some of the central concepts, arguments, questions, and controversies at the heart of the competing and conflicting approaches to social theory and theorizing.

I use the studies analyzed in *Exploring the Roots of Social Theory* as examples of the theorizing that underlies all studies of social life, even those directed at general readers and written by authors who don't consider themselves theorists. I try to connect these examinations of theorizing to other social science courses. Chapter 3, for instance, contrasts how concepts like history culture, class, caste, race, and gender are defined in introductory texts with how they are employed in the studies examined here. In Chapter 4, I show how Durkheim and Weber, as part of their debate with Marx, developed new ways of studying social life. I also demonstrate how Murray, Alexander, Wolf, and Kovach use methods and data to address the social and intellectual problems their studies address. The comparison of Murray's *Coming Apart* with Alexander's *The New Jim Crow* demonstrates the difference between how consensus and conflict theories are described in introductory texts and how social analysts use these theories in their studies. The analysis of the works of Murray,

Alexander, and Wolf demonstrate how the topic of economic and social inequality is theorized differently by different analysts in different studies. The comparison of Murray's study with Alexander's also provides a vehicle for an examination of the nature of objectivity and the role of ideology in social studies.

The comparison of how Murray, Alexander, and Wolf use history provides an opportunity for a discussion of how historians "do" history, and the different ways social scientists use what historians do. The comparison of these studies also illustrates various possible objects of social studies analysis—a particular society, a particular kind of society, or the interconnections between nation states existing within a global economy.

In Chapter 11, I use T. S. Kuhn's (1962) concept of paradigm to examine the relationship between the social and natural sciences. I argue that Murray, Alexander, and Wolf operate within the same paradigm, and employ the same set of theoretical concepts, connections between concepts, data sources, and techniques, to paint very different pictures of social life. While I don't employ the terms, instructors using this chapter might well point out that this paradigm is often referred to as positivist or post-positivist. I argue that while this paradigm may be dominant in the contemporary social sciences, it is not the only or necessarily the best approach to the study of human social life.

In Chapter 12, I contrast the paradigm within which Murray, Alexander, and Wolf operate with that Margaret Kovach describes in *Indigenous Methodologies*. I use this contrast to introduce the possibility of different ways of knowing and studying human social life. Kovach uses aspects of feminism, phenomenology, critical theory, and Marxism as a decolonizing lens, a way of moving from Western to non-Western ways of knowing. This provides an opening for the discussion and evaluation of these alternative forms of theorizing.

In Chapter 13, I bring together in summary fashion what the previous chapters have covered. I provide a step-by-step guide to how to uncover, describe, and evaluate the theorizing that underlies social studies, and to construct a research project proposal as way to begin your own theorizing.

I conclude by trying to demonstrate the contributions good theorizing can and has made to promoting positive social change. I also point out the issues students are likely to face if they decide to participate in social movements directed at advancing positive social change.

I designed *Exploring the Roots of Social Theory and Inquiry* to be accompanied by other book(s) or readings. My hope is that students, with the guidance of their instructors, might use the analysis of the studies I cover here as examples to guide them in uncovering, describing, and evaluating the theorizing that underlies other studies. The kind of accompanying readings that might be used of course are up to you. You know your students best and you know what objectives you want to achieve in your course. I hope you and your students find *Exploring the Roots of Social Theory and Inquiry* useful in making sense of the sense social scientists try to make of social life.

INTRODUCTION

SUGGESTIONS TO STUDENTS AS TO HOW THEY MIGHT USE THIS BOOK

It is customary to acquire the skills and knowledge required to systematically study social life by majoring in a social science in a university. Social science is as much craft as science and the practice of this craft requires imagination as well as knowledge and skill. The best way to acquire the skill and knowledge necessary to practice this craft is to carefully study the work of skilled crafts people and to begin to practice it yourself under their tutelage. This book is designed to help you do both things.

THEORIZING

I call the application of the knowledge, skill, methodology, and imagination employed to address social and intellectual problems theorizing. The first objective of this book is to demonstrate how to uncover, describe, and evaluate the theorizing that underlies any thoughtful social study. I have tried to show how this can be done through an analysis of four such studies: *Coming Apart* by Charles Murray (2012), *The New Jim Crow* by Michelle Alexander (2012), *The XX Factor* by Alison Wolf (2013), and *Indigenous Methodologies* by Margaret Kovach (2009). I selected these works because they are on topics of importance and interest, covered from widely different perspectives. I try to uncover, describe, and evaluate the theorizing present in these works in a way anyone with a basic understanding of a social science can understand.

THEORIZING AND PAINTING PICTURES

I compare social theorizing to painting a picture. The pictures the authors of these works construct are conceptions, viewpoints, and analyses of how the social world looks and works. They are attempts to address particular intellectual and social problems. The authors argue that the problems they address exist because the world looks and works the way they say it does. To solve these problems, they argue, the social world needs to look and work differently. It is through the analysis and evaluation of these works that I try to show how social scientists try to make sense of social life. Theorizing, as I view it, is the attempt to address social and intellectual problems in a systematic way.

LEARNING FROM EXAMPLES OF SOCIAL THEORIZING

You don't need to read the books analyzed here to understand the analysis. These works were selected as examples of the kinds of books any thoughtful student of social life *could* (and probably *should)* read. Instructors using this book might select one or a group of readings to read along with *Exploring the Roots of Social Theory and Inquiry.* To get the most out of this book, you should try to analyze and evaluate the selected reading(s) the way the works here are analyzed.

ANALYZING AND DOING SOCIAL THEORIZING

In addition to showing you how to uncover, describe, and evaluate the theorizing contained in social studies, *Exploring Social Theory* is designed show you how to theorize on a topic of your own choosing. In addition to review questions, each chapter ends with suggested assignments and further readings designed to guide you step by step in doing your own theorizing. (My advice is that you let your instructor decide if you need to do any of this further reading.) Using the studies analyzed in *Exploring Social Theory and Inquiry* as examples, and completing the assignments at the end of each chapter, should provide you with a good start at learning how social scientists attempt to address social and intellectual problems, and how you can systematically address problems of interest to you.

CURIOSITIES, CONCERNS, AND PASSIONS: YOURS AND THOSE OF THE AUTHORS WHOSE STUDIES YOU ANALYZE

In Chapter 1, I ask you to remember why you began to study social life. What first piqued your curiosity about the way we live? What social problems concerned you? What social injustices aroused your passions? You might begin the effort of making sense of social life by making sense of yourself and the reasons, motives, and purposes (or curiosities, concerns, and passions) that first brought you to the systematic study of social life. In this chapter I point out that the authors of the studies examined in *Exploring Social Theory* were driven by their own curiosities, concerns, and passions. Understanding studies of social life begins with understanding the curiosities, concerns, and passions that motivated their authors to write them.

SOCIAL POSITIONS AND SOCIAL STANCES: HOW WE VIEW THE WORLD AND THE PLACE FROM WHICH WE VIEW IT

When we attempt to understand and evaluate how social analysts study human social life, we need to keep in mind that these analysts occupy particular positions within the social world and that their work embodies particular stances toward that world. They have their reasons for studying social life and studying it the way they do. We too occupy a position within the social world, and we too have our reasons for studying social life. We need to be conscious of the position from which we come at our analysis of the analysts whose work we are attempting to understand. We should also be aware of our own motivations when we do our own theorizing.

THE SOCIOLOGICAL IMAGINATION

Social study starts with curiosity, concern, and passion, but imagination moves the study along. C. Wright Mills (1959) called this sociological imagination. We use our sociological imagination to make connections: between our private troubles and public issues; between our troubles and those of those around us; between people like us and other people very different from us; between actions and the social context within which those actions take place; between our own time and place and other times and other places. After reading Chapter 1 you should reflect on the curiosities, concerns, and passions that have motivated you to systematically study social life. You should reflect on your life and how you have attempted to make sense of it. This would also be a good time to select a reading or readings to analyze.

Moving from Social Topics to Social and Intellectual Problems: Using Concepts, Data, and Methods to Construct Pictures of Social Life That Depict Social and Intellectual Problems

In Chapter 2, I suggest a way to understand how social scientists try to make of sense of social life. Following Michael Baxandall (1985), I compare the effort to make such sense to what artists do when they paint a picture or what engineers do when they design and construct a bridge or building. The authors of well-conceived social studies use their imagination as well as their curiosities, concerns, and passions to transform a social topic (the family, deviance, race, class, gender) into a social or intellectual problem. They then formulate an educated guess (a rough hypothesis) as to the causes of this problem. Next, they construct a picture of social life based on their hypothesis that shows why the problem they have selected exists. The main tools and materials they use to construct this picture are theoretical concepts, research methods, and data. They use their imagination to employ these tools and materials to design a pattern of connections among social phenomena. This pattern of connections is their picture of social reality. They argue, in effect, that the problem they address exists because the social world looks and works the way they say it does in the picture they have drawn.

Doing Social Theorizing: Reflection on Your Stance Toward the Social World and the Role Your Life Experiences Played in the Development of That Stance

Selecting a Topic on Which to Theorize

After you have completed reading the second chapter of *Exploring Social Theory* you should reflect further on the curiosities, concerns, and passions that made you decide to systematically study social life. What role did your life experiences play in this decision? Do you have a stance, perspective, or ideology that frames your study of social life? What social topics most interest you? Select one of those topics and use your sociological imagination as well as your curiosities, concerns, and passions to transform the topic you select into a social or intellectual problem.

Using concepts as tools

Because theoretical concepts are important tools we employ to paint our pictures of social life, in Chapter 3 I try to show the difference between how theoretical concepts are defined in introductory social science texts and how they are used in social studies. Theoretical concepts are tools we use to make sense of social life; they aren't descriptions of social life. History, for example, isn't "one damn thing after another," it is a way of making sense of the past and the role the past plays in the present.

Because they are central to the studies analyzed in *Exploring Social Theory*, I concentrate on distinguishing how the concepts of **history, culture, class, caste, race**, and **gender** are used in these studies from how they are defined in introductory texts. I make the point that there is often a difference in how concepts are defined and how they are used. After reading this chapter you should begin to identify the major theoretical concepts used in the reading(s) you have chosen to analyze. You should also think about what concepts you think you would employ in your own theorizing.

Methods: Approaches to the study of social life and of using techniques to construct data

The study of theory is often separated from the study of methods, and methods are divided into kinds: qualitative and quantitative. Most social science programs have separate courses for each. Too often, theory courses are unconnected from methods courses, and qualitative methods courses are unconnected from quantitative methods courses. Addressing social or intellectual problems (theorizing) requires an understanding of how to use concepts as tools and method as a way of using techniques (both qualitative and quantitative) to construct data. Just as concepts aren't descriptions of reality but tools used to make sense of it, so data isn't so much discovered as created. Methods are both approaches to the study of social life and ways of using quantitative and qualitative techniques to create data, which is then used to make sense of social reality. Chapter 4 isn't designed to teach you how to use techniques for creating data (that's what methods courses are for). It is instead designed to show you how social scientists employ methods, methodological techniques, and data to address social and intellectual problems. In doing so, I hope to show you the value of methods in making sense of social life.

Uncovering, Describing, and Evaluating the Theorizing That Underlies Social Studies: Examples

The next six chapters of *Exploring Social Theory* consist of detailed analyses of three of the four studies I have chosen as examples of studies of social life. While the studies are interesting and important in their own right, we are most interested in how the authors of these studies have constructed them. We are interested in how they theorize. I analyze these studies in order to show you how to make sense of such studies and how to do your own theorizing.

Charles Murray's Coming Apart

In *Coming Apart*, Charles Murray uses **history, culture,** and **class** to try to demonstrate how over time America has gone from a society with a widely shared civic culture to one torn apart by the emergence of two new social classes. We are interested in how (and how well) Murray uses the concepts of history, culture, and class along with a wide variety of statistical data to paint two pictures of American social life: one of American life in the early 1960s; the other of American life as it exists now.

Michelle Alexander's *The New Jim Crow*

In *The New Jim Crow*, Michelle Alexander uses the concepts of **history, caste, race,** and **class** to construct a very different picture of how American social life has developed over time. Alexander uses history differently than does Murray, and for different purposes. Alexander wants to show that, since America's beginnings, upper-class whites have used race and racism to construct different forms of racialized caste to control and oppress African Americans. She wants to show how slavery, Jim Crow segregation, and the mass incarceration of poor black men are different forms of racialized caste.

Alison Wolf's *The XX Factor*

In *The XX Factor*, Alison Wolf uses **history** and the concepts of **gender, caste, class,** and **developed society** to show how well-educated, well-paid professional women have escaped the gender caste while most other women have remained within it.

In doing so, she argues, these women have unwittingly increased social inequality and brought into question the usefulness of **"women"** as a theoretical concept. The lives of women in developed societies, she argues, are so different it no longer makes sense to analyze them through the use of the same concept.

Is It Possible to Think About and Experience the World Differently?

In Chapter 10, I suggest that though there are wide ideological differences separating the works of Murray, Alexander, and Wolf, they use many of the same concepts, and connect the concepts they use in many of the same ways to address many of the same questions. While they give very different answers to the questions they ask, they operate within what T. S. Kuhn called the same **intellectual paradigm**. While I don't call this paradigm positivist or post-positivist, your instructor may, and if they do, they won't be wrong. This paradigm is currently the dominant one in contemporary social science but it is far from the only one. It is possible to use different concepts, data, and methods to establish different connections between social phenomena and to ask different questions about social life. In other words, it is possible to make different kinds of sense of social life and make that sense differently.

Margaret Kovach's *Indigenous Methodologies*

In Chapter 11, I analyze Margaret Kovach's *Indigenous Methodologies* to illustrate this point. Kovach argues that it is possible to understand the sense indigenous people make of their own lives in their own terms—terms very different than those employed by Murray, Alexander, Wolf, and many other Western analysts. In doing so she raises the very contentious philosophical issue of whether or not it is possible to think differently. If different people living in different times, places, and social situations think differently, how can people who think differently understand each other? If, as Kovach suggests, indigenous peoples think differently than Westerners, is it possible for Westerners to understand how indigenous peoples think, and to learn important things from the way they think?

OVERVIEW OF HOW TO ANALYZE AND DO SOCIAL THEORIZING

In Chapter 13, I try to bring what this book covers together in summary fashion. I provide a step-by-step overview of how to understand the sense social analysts try to make of social life. I also provide a step-by-step overview of how to begin to make your own sense of some aspect of social life. *Exploring Social Theory and Inquiry* is an introduction to how to uncover, describe, and evaluate the theorizing that underlies studies of social life. It is also an introduction to how to make your own sense of how we live and how we live together. In other words, it is an introduction to how to uncover, describe, and evaluate the theorizing of social scientists and how to begin to do your own theorizing.

SOCIAL THEORIZING AND SOCIAL CHANGE

In the concluding chapter I try to make the case that good theorizing can be a powerful instrument in promoting social change. I also attempt to point out the ethical dilemmas and difficulties you will face if you participate in movements of social change. I argue that while changing the world involves more than just attempting to understand it, no responsible person should try to change a world they haven't attempted to understand.

CHAPTER 1

FULFILLING THE PROMISE: INFUSING CURIOSITY, CONCERN, AND PASSION WITH SOCIOLOGICAL IMAGINATION

It is not theoretical questions that first interest people in social study. It is curiosity about social life and how it works; concern for social problems and how to solve them; passion against social injustices and a desire to right them. If social study dampens this curiosity, concern, and passion, it betrays you. If social study shows you how to harness and employ that curiosity, concern, and passion, it does you a service.

CURIOSITY

When you study social life in a systematic and disciplined manner, it's important to periodically remind yourself why you do so. How did your journey start, and why do you continue it? Such journeys usually begin with curiosity. Why are things the way they are? Have they always been that way? Are they this way everywhere? How might they be different? Peter Berger (1963, 19), in his classic *Invitation to Sociology*, points to "the curiosity that grips any sociologist in front of a closed door behind which there are human voices. If he [or she] is a good sociologist, [she or] he will want to open that door, to understand these voices. Behind each closed door he [or she] will anticipate some new facet of human life not yet perceived and understood."

The limits of all of our experiences are such that the recognition of changes in our life and that of those around us don't necessarily tell us about what's happening to people outside our immediate vicinity. Are the changes happening to us peculiar to our neighborhood, region, class, ethnic or racial grouping, nation, or area of the world? When did these changes begin? How long have they been going on? Where will they lead? This is the curiosity out of which an interest in social study begins.

Margaret Kovach's interest in social life began with curiosity about her own origins. Her education was a portal to self-discovery. Her birth parents were Plains Cree and Salteaux. Her adopted parents were Eastern European. "I was a native kid who grew up round and about a small rural Saskatchewan town. I was loved but conflicted, questioning where I belonged, trying to stay at distances yet needing connection" (2009, 5).

Alison Wolf's upbringing was very different from that of Margaret Kovach, but of course for her, as for all of us, it was "normal." She "grew up in prosperous, peaceful southern England ... where it was simply taken for granted that we would all go on to college ... because it was normal for my school and for my friends, only years later did I realize how few women, even in our baby-boomer generations, did academic, let alone post-graduate degrees or how few had done so previously" (2013, xi). It was only later that she realized that hers was a "hinge generation." "My generation didn't see this coming. But then, as students or young professionals, we didn't or couldn't survey what society as a whole was doing. What was normal was what we, as privileged sub-group, did" (xii). It is only now that she is able to put what was happening to her and women like her into a global social context. It is only now that she realizes that hers was a hinge generation (xv).

The curiosity that initiates our interest in social life is usually mixed with an "unhealthy" dose of skepticism. Again, Peter Berger: "The first wisdom of sociology is this—things are not what they seem" (1963, 23). I say "unhealthy" because such curiosity and skepticism isn't always helpful in everyday situations. Much of our everyday interactions with others is based on routine. We do the same things in same way, every day. We rarely think about what is involved in taking the bus, buying groceries, riding the elevator, or hanging out with our friends. We don't have to think about how these things happen or what it takes to make them happen. We just do them.

Indeed, for everyday encounters with others to come off successfully, it is important not to think too carefully or deeply about what is really going on. We accept that the people we interact with are who they appear to be. They, in turn, accept the self we present to them as the real us. Irving Goffman (1967) tells us that this kind of mutual acceptance seems to be a basic structural feature of interaction, especially the interaction of face-to-face talk. Think too carefully about our routines as we perform them, question them too deeply, and they will be hard to do.

What might be unhealthy and destructive in everyday life can be important for the student of social life. The surface of social life is rarely, if ever, all there is. Beneath that surface are layers and layers of social meaning. Our everyday routines are rarely as simple as they appear. They are often not as secure as they seem. The tacit knowledge, practical consciousness, and unreflective negotiation that goes into riding the bus, having a meal in a restaurant, riding the elevator, buying groceries, or hanging out with our friends is the object of study of a whole branch of sociology known as **ethnomethodology**.

Ethnomethodology

Study of how everyday life interactions happen. Endomethodologists view everyday life interactions like going to the grocery store, eating at a restaurant, taking a bus ride as artful accomplishments involving shared background knowledge, tacit understandings and negotiation between the participants in such interactions.

Figure 1.1: Ethnomethodology

Often our curiosity is piqued by something that seems out of the ordinary in our routine. As a civil rights attorney, Michelle Alexander saw her job as resisting attacks on affirmative action. One day she was rushing to catch a bus when she "noticed a sign stapled to a telephone pole that screamed in large bold print: 'The Drug War is the New Jim Crow'" (2012, 3). Her first reaction was that the comparison was absurd. Yet it made her curious.

Concern

Oh – something ain't right
Oh – something ain't right

—"Something Ain't Right," David Byrnes

Sometimes the desire to systematically study social life begins with the feeling or conviction that "something ain't right." The charge for riding the bus doubles and the service is reduced. The price of groceries rises dramatically. Our eyes fix on the people busing tables and washing dishes at the restaurant where we are having a meal. Thinking about their lives spoils the meal. Rowdy kids cut in front of an elderly woman in line for the elevator. When she complains, they push her down and laugh. Everyone else in line pretends not to notice. Our routines are interrupted. Things don't seem to be working the way we think they should or the way they used to. We wonder what has gone wrong, why things cost so much, why some people make so little, and why other people behave so badly.

Charles Murray (2012, 288) remembers that when he was growing up in the 1940s and 1950s there was a code governing the behavior of "gentlemen":

I understood the code for males to go something like this: To be a man means that you are brave, loyal and true. When you are in the wrong you own up and take your punishment. You don't take advantage of women.

As a husband, you support and protect your wife and children. You are gracious in victory and a good sport in defeat. Your word is your bond. It's not whether you win or lose but how you play the game. When the ship goes down, you put the women and children in the lifeboats and wave good-bye with a smile.

Murray admits that the above is crammed with clichés. But, he argues, "they were clichés precisely because boys understood that this was the way they were supposed to behave. ... The code of the American gentleman has collapsed, just as the parallel code of the American lady has collapsed" (2012, 288–89). He thinks the collapse of this code is a bad thing. He's concerned about why it has collapsed and what the consequences of its collapse will be.

Passion

Something about the way things are doesn't seem just or fair. Parents sometimes rhetorically ask their kids, "Who said that life was fair?" They add, "When you get older you'll understand." For some of us, our parents' words aren't enough. Just because things aren't fair doesn't mean that we have to accept that unfairness. When we get older we still don't understand why social injustice has to exist. We want to know how social injustices can be addressed. Just because life isn't fair doesn't mean it can't be made fairer and more just.

In the Prologue of *Indigenous Methodologies*, Margaret Kovach says, "I get angry about the racism that Indigenous people experience. I am writing this here because it drives my work. ... The writing comes from the heart, it comes from who I am and all that I am. ... It comes from my own need and longing to engage with my Nehiyaw and Salteaux ancestry, and to say to my academic world that my culture counts" (2009, 5–8).

In the Preface to *The New Jim Crow*, Michelle Alexander (2012) identifies the readers for whom she has written her book:

People who care deeply about racial justice but who, for any number of reasons, do not yet appreciate the magnitude of the crisis faced by communities of color as a result of mass incarceration. In other words, I am writing this book for people like me—the person I was ten years ago. I am also writing it for another audience—those who have been struggling to persuade their friends, neighbors, relatives, teachers, coworkers, or political representatives that something is eerily familiar about the way our criminal justice system operates, something that looks and feels a lot like an era that we supposedly left behind, but who have lacked the facts and data to back up their claims. It is my hope and prayer that this book empowers you and allows you to speak with greater conviction, credibility and courage.

Charles Murray directs his book *Coming Apart* at a very different audience, and has very different things to say than does Michelle Alexander. But he too is passionate about what he perceives as prevailing social wrongs, including the dysfunctionality and irresponsibility of the new American upper class:

> Personally and as families its members are successful. But they have abrogated their responsibility to set and promulgate standards. The most powerful and successful members of their class increasingly trade on the perks of their privileged positions without regard to the seemliness of that behavior. The members of the new upper class are active politically, but when it comes to using their positions to help sustain the republic in day-to-day life, they are AWOL. (2012, 294)

USING YOUR SOCIOLOGICAL IMAGINATION TO MAKE CONNECTIONS

If interest in the systematic study of social life begins with curiosity, skepticism, concern, and passion, it doesn't end there. Curiosity needs to be sated; skepticism and suspicion justified or allayed; social wrongs righted. This requires the acquisition of particular kinds of knowledge and the use of a particular form of imagination—what C. Wright Mills (1959) called the **sociological imagination**.

By the sociological imagination, Mills meant that quality of mind which enables people who possess it to make connections between personal troubles and social issues. Troubles occur within or between individuals sharing the same immediate social environment. Losing a job; doing badly at school; failing at marriage or a relationship; even committing a crime, getting arrested, and being put in prison can certainly be understood in very immediate and personal terms. People lose jobs all the time because they screw up at work or can't get along with their bosses and coworkers. We sometimes do badly at school because we are too lazy to study or would rather party. People sometimes treat their partners with a lack of respect and fail to put the time and attention into a relationship necessary to make it work. Sometimes it really is our fault.

Often, however, it isn't—or isn't completely. When businesses close or stop hiring, when millions of people get laid off and you lose your job, that isn't your fault. When the dropout rates in urban public schools rise and the academic performance of the students who remain drops precipitately, something more is at work than student laziness. When the divorce rate rises dramatically, clearly more is at work than couples failing to make the compromises necessary for a successful marriage. When people decide to drive while drunk or stoned, they place themselves and others at risk. Surely, they should be held accountable for their actions. Yet the need for accountability doesn't explain why some people are held more accountable than others. While people of all races appear to use and sell illegal drugs at about the same rate, black men are imprisoned for drug offenses at rates twenty to fifty times greater than those of white men (Alexander 2012, 7). Sometimes personal problems are connected to public issues.

"An issue is a public matter: some value cherished by publics is felt to be threatened. Often there is a debate about what that value really is and about what it is that really threatens it" (Mills 1959, 8). Murray thinks that the core values, the "founding virtues" that made America great, indeed exceptional—industriousness, honesty, marriage, and religiosity—are being threatened (2012,130). Alexander thinks that the incarceration of poor African American males for drug offenses is not about an increase in crime or drug abuse. It is rather the result of "a stunningly comprehensive and well-disguised system of racialized social control that functions in a manner strikingly similar to Jim Crow" (2012, 4).

Certainly, making connections between personal troubles and social issues requires gathering the relevant facts, and exercising our reasoning capacity to make sense of those facts. But making sense of the social world requires more than facts and reasoning. It requires a quality of mind that will help us "to use information and develop reason in order to achieve lucid summations of what is going on in the world and of what is happening in [ourselves]" (Mills 1959, 5). When we do this, we use our sociological imagination to theorize.

THEORY AND THEORIZING: A DIFFERENT WAY OF LOOKING AT SOCIAL THEORY

Too often, in my view, social theories and the work of social theorists are separated from both what the theories are about, and how social theorists employ those theories to make sense of the social world. In an important sense, all thoughtful students of social life are theorists. They create and present theoretical constructions, pictures of social reality, as explanations for social problems. These problems, they argue, exist because the social world looks and works like this. To solve these problems, they argue, the social world needs to look different and to work differently.

EXAMPLES OF THEORIZING

Here I have selected four works as examples of theorizing. I don't assume that the readers of this book will have read the studies analyzed in it, only that they could read and understand them, and works like them. The studies analyzed here focus on key contemporary social phenomena—history, race, culture, class, gender, and indigenous peoples. They do so, however, from widely different perspectives. Charles Murray is an unabashed man of the right and his book has been influential in conservative circles. Michelle Alexander is a proud woman of the left and her book is very influential in the liberal-left community. Alison Wolf is an accomplished British economist, educator, and journalist. Her book does one of the things important books on social life should do—examines the unexpected and potentially negative consequences of positive social developments. The subtitle of her well-reviewed book is "How the Rise of Working Women Has Created a Far Less Equal World." Margaret Kovach is a member of the Plains Cree and Salteaux peoples of the Great Plains in southern Saskatchewan. Hers is the only book of the four which could be considered a work of theory, but the indigenous theories and methods she discusses are not ones ordinarily covered in books or courses on theory.

I will try to show that each of these works involves theorizing. Each work is an attempt to address a particular social or intellectual problem. Each author begins by identifying something that they believe is out of order in the social world. They then present a picture of a social life that illustrates the nature of the problem they have identified. Finally, they show how that picture would have to be changed for the problem to be successfully addressed.

In this book, I will attempt to uncover, describe, and evaluate the theorizing that underlies these studies. **While you're reading this book, you should do two things. First, in conjunction with your instructor, select a study, reading, or readings that stimulate your curiosity, concern, and passion. Uncover, describe, and evaluate the theorizing that underlies the study you have chosen as you read this book. Second, use your curiosity, concern, passion, and sociological imagination to show how you might do your own theorizing. I don't ask that you construct a study; only that you write a proposal describing the kind of study you would like to do, had you the time and resources.**

At the end of each chapter I will give short assignments which will allow you to gradually uncover, describe, and evaluate the theorizing in the study you have chosen, and to demonstrate how you might do your own theorizing. If you complete the assignments at the end of each chapter, and use the explanation and analysis of the studies I provide here as examples of how to uncover, describe, analyze, and perform social theorizing, I think you will have accomplished a great deal.

STUDY QUESTIONS

1. What is the sociological imagination? What do I mean by the term "social theorizing?"
2. Identify something in social life about which you are curious.
3. Identify a social problem about which you are concerned.
4. Identify a form of social injustice that troubles you, and about which you are passionate.
5. Describe how these curiosities, concerns, and passions are linked to your life and the lives of those around you.

SUGGESTED ASSIGNMENT

1. Write a short essay (500 to 750 words) identifying one aspect of social life about which you are curious, one social problem about which you are concerned, and one form of social injustice about which you are passionate. Describe how these curiosities, concerns, and passions are related to your own life experiences.

SUGGESTED FURTHER READINGS

Berger, Peter. 1963. *Invitation to Sociology*, 164–177 (Sociology as a Humanistic Discipline). Garden City, New York: Doubleday Anchor Books.

Mills, C. Wright. 1959. *The Sociological Imagination*, 3–25 (The Promise). New York: Oxford University Press.

CHAPTER 2

THEORY AND THEORIZING: HOW TO UNCOVER THE THEORIZING IN A SOCIAL STUDY

SO MANY THEORIES, SO LITTLE TIME

There are many ways of conceiving and categorizing contemporary social theories. There are positivist and post-positivist theories; normative analytic theories; ideographic, nomothetic, and critical theories; Marxist theories; structuralist, post-structuralist, modernist and post-modernist theories; structural functional and conflict theories; symbolic interactionist and rational choice theories; ethnomethodological and dramaturgical theories; grand theories and middle-level theories; macro, mezzo, and micro theories; feminist and queer theories.

Each of these kinds of theory has something to recommend it. Each has famous practitioners and adherents. The debate amongst their advocates has been prolonged and often acrimonious. The drawback to classifying theories into kinds, in my view (in addition to the difficulty of differentiating one kind from another), is that such classifications separate theory from what it is a theory of. Shouldn't a theory be a theory of something?

FROM THEORIES AND THEORISTS TO THEORIZING

Here my objective is to introduce you to the **theorizing** that underlies studies of social life. In taking this approach, I have deliberately not attempted to provide a comprehensive overview of the various forms of social theory listed above. Instead, I have tried to uncover the theorizing that social analysts employ in their studies of social life.

RECONNECTING THEORY WITH THE STUDIES THEY ARE THEORIES OF

One of my key objectives is to reconnect theories with the studies they emerge from. I do this by examining particular social studies and attempting to identify the theorizing that takes place within them. I look at how the authors of these studies use their **sociological imaginations, curiosities, concerns, and passions to transform social topics into social or intellectual problems**. The authors of these studies attempt to depict these problems by **making connections** between different aspects of social life, **using these connections to construct a picture of social life, and giving an account of how it looks and works. Constructing these pictures of social life and using those pictures as a way of depicting intellectual and social problems is one way to conceive of theorizing.** Uncovering, describing, and evaluating this kind of theorizing is what I want to concentrate on in this book.

The authors of the studies analyzed here approach their topics from very different perspectives. Each author has their own particular curiosities, concerns, and passions that they bring to the topics their studies address. Each views the social world from a different ideological perspective. My objective is neither to critique their ideological perspectives nor to question the legitimacy of their curiosities, concerns, and passions. Instead, I want to identify and describe the role theorizing plays in each author's attempt to make sense of social life. My hope is that introducing theorizing in this way will demonstrate its relevance to social study.

Elements of Social Theorizing

- Curiosities, concerns and passions
- Identify the topic of the study
- Use sociological imagination to transform the topic into social or intellectual problem
- Description of the problem
- Construct an hypothesis as to why the problem the study addresses exists.
- Select the major concepts, data and methods to be employed in the study
- Design the pattern of connections between social phenomena which depicts the problem the study addresses
- Show how the social world would have to change for the problem to be solved

Figure 2.1: Steps involved in social theorizing

USING CONCEPTS, DATA, AND METHODS TO CONSTRUCT PICTURES OF SOCIAL LIFE

As I suggested in the last chapter, social study starts with curiosity about social life and how it works; concern for social problems and how to solve them; and passion against social injustices and a desire to right them. Sating that curiosity, solving those problems, righting those injustices requires an understanding of the social world and how it works. That understanding requires mastery of theoretical concepts, the ability to find and use data, and the ability to use research methodologies or at least to understand the role of research methodologies in the construction of data. The more materials you have at your disposal, the more tools you are able to use, the better the picture you can construct of the social world. The better your picture is, the sounder your understanding of social problems will be; the sounder your understanding of social problems, the better your chances of solving them.

Comprehending theoretical concepts and mastering research methodologies are daunting tasks. Trying to learn theory and methods in the abstract can dampen the curiosity, concern, and passion that interested you in social studies to begin with. I think the risk of such dampening can be minimized and the process of acquiring a theoretical vocabulary and research skills can be aided by **looking systematically at how theoretical concepts and research skills are used in particular social studies**. The studies we will systematically examine here are attempts to address particular social or intellectual problems. The depictions of these problems take the form of pictures of the social world and how it works. These pictures are constructed with theoretical concepts and data, and through the application of research methodologies. The hope is that the examination of these pictures and how they are constructed will not only aid you in mastering theorizing and methods, but demonstrate the usefulness of both as well.

THE CONSTRUCTION OF PURPOSEFUL OBJECTS

I want to begin by looking at these pictures of social life in the same way Michael Baxandall (1985) looked at the construction of purposeful objects in *Patterns of Intention*. Baxandall is an art critic and historian. Not surprisingly, amongst the "purposeful objects" he examines are paintings—Picasso's *Portrait of Kahnweiler*, Chardin's *A Lady Taking Tea* and Piero della Francesca's *The Baptism of Christ*. What is surprising is his comparison of the construction of these paintings with the construction in 1890 of the Forth Bridge, which connects Scotland to England at Queensferry. Baxandall doesn't suggest that the construction of paintings and bridges are the same. There are important differences. But in both cases, "the making of a picture or other historical artifact is a man [or woman] addressing a problem of which his [or her] product is a finished and concrete solution. To understand it we try to reconstruct both the specific problem it was designed to solve and the specific circumstances out of which he [or she] was addressing it" (Baxandall 1985, 15).

Building Bridges, Painting Paintings, and Designing Social Studies

Both bridges and paintings begin with a charge—build a bridge! Paint a painting! But engineers don't construct just any kind of bridge out of any kind of materials with any kind of design and place it anywhere. Artists don't make any kind of painting out of anything that happens to be at hand. Engineers who build bridges and artists who paint paintings have what Baxandall called a brief, as well as a charge. The brief consists of the particular conditions under which a particular bridge or painting is constructed. In constructing a bridge or painting, an engineer or an artist addresses "objective problems within a circumstantial frame of other facts that affect his [or her] perception of the problem" (Baxandall 1985, 30).

Composing a social study isn't the same as building a bridge or painting a painting, but some of the same elements and processes are at work. I don't think I would be completely wrong to suggest that a social analyst is part engineer and part artist. Social analysts face similar challenges in constructing their pictures to those faced by artists constructing theirs. Painters face the problem of representing three-dimensional reality on a two-dimensional surface. "How is one to represent things and persons ... recalcitrantly three-dimensional, and yet also positively acknowledge the two-dimensional plane of the canvas?" (Baxandall 1985, 44).

Paintings don't and can't reproduce the objects they paint. There is a clear difference between a painting and its subject. Artists must address and resolve the tensions that result from this in their works—the tensions between their medium of forms, colors, and distances visually perceived and pictorially deployed (Baxandall 1985, 47).

Pictures of the Social World as Theoretical Constructions

Constructing a picture of the social world and how it works involves the resolution of similar tensions. These pictures aren't life-sized models or X-ray images of the social world. The pictures of the social world analysts construct are conceptions, particular ways of seeing and analyzing it. Pictures of the social world are, in this sense, theoretical constructions and can be analyzed and evaluated as such.

MOVING FROM TOPIC TO PROBLEM

What Baxandall calls a charge, we will call a topic. Inequality, race, and the environment are social topics. While the selection of a topic is affected by the curiosities, concerns, and passions of the author of a study, the selection of the topic addressed in the study is also affected by the curiosities, concerns, and passions dominant in particular publics at the time the study is conceived and written. The topics addressed by the authors of articles in academic journals are more specialized than those addressed here. Still, to have the studies that address topics published in academic journals, they must have a readership (though a more specialized one) that shares their interest in the topic and how it might be addressed.

Amongst the topics addressed by the authors of the social studies we will examine are inequality, race, gender, and indigenous peoples. But just as an engineer doesn't build just any bridge anywhere with anything, and a painter doesn't paint just any kind of painting, students of social life don't all address topics in the same way. They bring their own unique perspectives and preoccupations to bear on the topics they address. Each addresses his or her topic in their own particular way. Just as the engineer has a brief as well as a charge, so the social analyst takes a topic and transforms it into a problem in their own particular way.

ADDRESSING SOCIAL AND INTELLECTUAL PROBLEMS

Karl Popper (1976, 1988), a well-known philosopher of science, argued that systematic inquiry begins not with observations but with problems. Problems can take different forms. Social problems can be facets or aspects of the existing social world that seem troubling or wrong to us—war, hunger, pollution, or the violation of human rights. In order to adequately address social problems like these, social analysts must sometimes address intellectual problems related to them as well. While we know a great deal about the social world, there is even more about which we are ignorant or misinformed. We sometimes discover that some of what we think we know turns out to be wrong. The discovery of new facts indicates that what we thought true about an aspect of social life may well be false. It turns out that middle-class youth don't usually go to inner-city neighborhoods to buy drugs; they usually score their drugs in their own middle-class neighborhoods. The rise of highly educated, well-paid professional women might not be a victory for all women; it might just be a victory for highly educated, well-paid professional women.

It sometimes turns out that when we clearly state what we think we know about the social world, some of these statements contradict each other. Since statements can't be both true and false, some part of what we think we know must be false if the other part is to be true. We believe that when rates of unemployment go up, crime rates go up. During the great recession of 2008, the unemployment rate in the United States went dramatically up but the crime rate went down. What's wrong with this picture? If we are interested in social life, we should try to find out.

Intellectual problems are intimately connected to social problems. If some things we think we know about the social world turn out not to be true; if we discover that something we think we know about the social world appears to be contradicted by something else we think we know about the social world, then some of what we think we know may well be wrong. If we are able to eliminate the erroneous knowledge and replace it with more accurate knowledge, we may find that social problems that previously seemed insoluble have solutions.

USING CURIOSITY, CONCERN, PASSION, AND SOCIOLOGICAL IMAGINATION TO TRANSFORM TOPICS INTO PROBLEMS

Social analysts use their sociological imagination and their curiosities, concerns, and passions to transform topics into problems. Different analysts with different curiosities, concerns, and passions often transform the same topics into very different problems. They also conceive of similar problems differently. How they conceive of the problem they set for themselves is influenced by the particular angle of vision they take toward social life. The picture they create of social life is tailored to address the social problem they have set for themselves.

HOW SOCIAL ANALYSTS THEORIZE

Let us start with the following account of how social analysts theorize. An analyst theorizes that a given problem exists because the social world looks and works the way they say it does. The analyst further theorizes that for the problem to be solved, the social world needs to be altered so that it looks and works differently. Alternatively, an analyst might theorize that we are unable to solve or even properly address a given problem because the currently dominant view of the social world and how it works is fundamentally incomplete or wrong. The analyst might then further theorize that the social world actually looks and works differently. When we reconceive how the social world or some part of it looks and works in these different terms, the analyst theorizes, the real nature of the social problem is revealed, as are ways of solving it.

Thus, **the way we picture the world and how it works is not separate from the way we conceive of a problem**. Those aspects of social life about which we are curious, concerned, or passionate are part and parcel of how we conceive of social life and how it works. If we think that the way most people currently conceive of social life and how it works is wrong in some fundamental way and should be conceived of differently, our different conception of social life and how it works influences what we think needs to be changed to make things better.

TOOLS AND MATERIALS: CONCEPTS, METHODS, AND DATA

Like paintings and bridges, pictures of the social world are constructed by people using tools and materials. The most important of these tools and materials are theoretical concepts, particular methods of studying the social world and particular techniques for creating data. However, tools, materials, and methodologies don't create pictures of social reality by themselves. To create such pictures, analysts must choose their tools and materials carefully and employ them with creativity, skill, and imagination.

IDEOLOGY, ETHICS, AND THE DEVELOPMENT OF AN INFORMED PERSPECTIVE ON THE SOCIAL WORLD

The topics addressed in the four studies we will look at here—inequality, race, gender, and indigenous peoples—are certainly ones which have captured the public's attention. Each of the authors of these studies uses their sociological imagination to infuse these topics with their own particular curiosities, concerns, and passions, and to transform a topic into a social problem they have chosen to address.

IDEOLOGY: OUR PERSPECTIVE ON THE WORLD AND OUR POSITION IN IT

Ideology is an important factor in their (and our) selection of the problems they (we) choose to address and of the way they (we) conceive of these problems. There are almost as may ideologies as there are social theories. After surveying the many meanings of ideology, Karl Mannheim (1926, 116) concluded that ideology was simply "a certain way of looking at things."

Ideology is important because we don't just observe and analyze the social world; we live in it. Our position in the social world affects how we look at it. Our sociological imagination can broaden our perspective on the social world by connecting our own situation with those different from our own. Broadening our perspective may change it (or may not), but it won't eliminate perspective itself—nor should it. Our social situation and how we came to occupy it should contribute to our perspective on the world. Reflection on our position in the world and the life experiences that have helped make us who we are should be a major part of how we view social life.

REFLECTION ON THE WORLD AND HOW WE HAVE COME TO VIEW IT

An informed perspective must contain something more as well. To take an informed perspective on the world, we need to use our sociological imagination (and have a mastery of the necessary tools and materials) to identify the positions occupied by others in situations very different from our own. We need to be able to make the connections between the positions occupied by people in different life situations. We need to attempt to understand both the shared and individual components contributing to the social actions we and others take. We need to reflect on how we think people ought to live and how they ought to live together. An informed perspective should be informed by a social ethic that is the product of careful reflection.

Objectivity, Reflection, and Social Values

It is possible to argue, though I don't think persuasively, that social analysis should be non-ideological and value free. The argument goes something like this. As a citizen or individual, a social analyst is free to take particular ideological positions, but when doing social analysis he or she should leave ideological biases aside and concentrate on describing social life and how it works as he or she finds it.

Even if this form of objectivity were a good thing, would it be possible to take such a stance toward social life? I don't think so. Reflection on where we have come from, on our life situation and that of people like us, should influence the perspective we take on the world. Our view of the good life and the good society inevitably does and should influence how we view the forms of social life we examine. It determines what we look for when we examine social life and how we characterize what we see.

SEARCHING OUT INCONVENIENT FACTS AND UNEXPECTED CONSEQUENCES

That doesn't mean that social analysis shouldn't be objective. I think there is a difference between attempting to be value free and neutral when we look at the social world, and being objective. Being objective entails the recognition of the obligation to search for and recognize the unintended and unexpected consequences of the social changes we favor. Being objective means not ignoring or minimizing what Max Weber (1919, 147) called "inconvenient facts"—social phenomena we discover that run counter to the social phenomena we would expect to see given our ideological position. We have an obligation to seek out data that runs counter to what we would expect to find; to search for the negative effects of a social world formed more or less the way we wish it were; and to give a fair rendering of social studies that originate from an ideological perspective different from our own.

REFLEXIVITY

Let me end this chapter with a caution. Theorizing about social life is in an important sense theorizing about theorizing. When human beings act and interact, they are aware of what they are doing. Whether we get up in the morning or stay in bed, go to school or stay home and watch TV, quit a job or get a new one, hang out with one group of friends rather than another, we have our reasons. At a practical level, we have a view of social life and how it works. In that sense, we theorize about social life every day. Much of the theorizing we do as analysts is theorizing about this everyday theorizing.

> The sociologist has as a field of study phenomena which are already constituted as meaningful. The condition of "entry" into this field is getting to know what actors already know and have to know to go on in the daily activities of social life. The concepts that the sociological observers invent

are "second order" concepts in so far as they presume certain conceptual capabilities on the part of the actors to whose conduct they refer. (Giddens 1984, 284)

As we investigate the investigators, we should be conscious of what we are doing (and not doing) and be cognizant of the choices we are making (and the alternative choices we forebear) and our reasons for making them. We should be as consciously reflective about our own analysis as we are about that of the works we are analyzing.

Study Questions

1. What is social theorizing?
2. How is theorizing similar to bridge building and painting?
3. What tools and raw materials do social scientists employ to construct their pictures of social life?
4. What is an ideology? Do you have one? Can you describe it?
5. How did your life experiences help you develop your perspective on the social world?
6. Is it possible to be objective without being value free or neutral when we study the social world?
7. What do we mean by unexpected consequences and inconvenient facts?
8. In what sense are we what we study when we study social life? What are the implications of this?

Assignments

1. In consultation with your instructor, select a reading or readings, the theorizing in which you will uncover, describe, and analyze during the term.
2. Read the paper you have written on your curiosities, concerns, and passions, and the life experiences that shaped them. Use that paper to identify a topic of interest to you. Use your curiosities, concerns, passions, and sociological imagination to transform that topic into a social or intellectual problem you would like to address.

Suggested Further Readings

Baxandall, Michael. 1985. *Patterns of Intention*, 12–36 (The Historical Object: Benjamin Baker's Forth Bridge). New Haven, Connecticut: Yale University Press.

Popper, Karl. 1976. "The Logic of the Social Sciences." In *The Positivist Dispute in German Sociology*, edited by Theodor Adorno, Hans Albert, Ralf Dahrendorf, Jurgen Habermas, Harald Piolog and Karl Popper, 87–103. New York: Harper and Row.

Swedberg, Richard. *The Art of Theorizing*, 1–13 (Why Theorize and Can You Learn to Do It). Princeton: Princeton University Press.

CHAPTER 3

THEORETICAL CONCEPTS ARE TOOLS, NOT THINGS

USING AND DEFINING CONCEPTS

In this chapter I want to illustrate the differences between how theoretical concepts are defined in social science texts and how they are used in social studies. The theoretical concepts defined in texts often take on different meanings when they are actually used by social scientists to make sense of social life.

The most challenging part of introductory texts is the bewildering variety of terms they introduce. These terms are of necessity vaguely defined, because different professors use the terms differently. I don't say this to criticize introductory social science texts. Introducing basic terms is part of what introductory texts are charged with doing. Nor am I criticizing the professors who use theoretical concepts differently in different contexts to make different points. Quite the contrary: that is the way language, even the language of social studies, works.

For example, what I mean by theorizing differs somewhat depending on the point I am making when I use it. Of course, all these uses share a core similarity. Theorizing is never a kind of fruit or vegetable. It's always an attempt to make sense of social life. Sometimes, however, I define theorizing as the use of knowledge, skill, and imagination to construct explanations of social and intellectual problems. At other times, I compare what social analysts do when they theorize to what artists do when they paint. At still other times I emphasize the role of theorizing in making connections between different aspects of social life. While all these uses of the term theorizing resemble one another, none is exactly the same. What I mean by theorizing in each case is determined by what particular point I make when I do so. Similarly, what the authors of the studies we will be analyzing mean by history, culture, class, caste, and gender is determined by how they use these terms and the points they are trying to make when they do so.

History

It is no longer fashionable, as it once was, to search for **universal laws** governing all forms of social life. Almost all contemporary social analysts recognize that human social life has an historical dimension. If the role of the historian is "to give the past back its present," one of the roles of the social analyst is to give the present its past Rosanvallon 2007, 708.

Though all of the studies we will look at here have a historical dimension, they don't all use history in the same way. Charles Murray and Alison Wolf use history as a border, a zero point, establishing the limit in time before which the phenomena they study didn't exist in the form in which they study it (Foucault 1965, ix). Charles Murray's zero point in *Coming Apart* is the assassination of President John Kennedy on November 22, 1963. He draws a picture of the United States as he sees it existing at that point in time, and then distinguishes that from the United States he sees existing now. His argument is that the past of the United States' present begins in the early 1960s. *Coming Apart* is "about an evolution in American society that has taken place since November 21 [sic], 1963, leading to the formation of classes that are different in kind and in the degree of separation from anything that the nation has ever known" (Murray 2012, 11).

Alison Wolf's zero point in *The XX Factor* is December, 1802, when Jane Austen broke off her engagement to Harris Bigg-Wither. Age 27 at the time, Austen was unlikely to receive another marriage offer. She had no independent income. "She was quite consciously depriving herself of everything that offered women status and security, namely marriage and children" (Wolf 2013, ix). Wolf's book is about contemporary elite women who, eight generations later, can't imagine such choices. "It is about their lives and about the choices that face them ... different from those ofAusten's time, far more extensive, but choices none the less" (ix).

Michelle Alexander uses history in a different way than do Murray and Wolf. Instead of establishing a zero point, Alexander uses history as a way of making comparisons in what she sees as a common element, a racialized system of social control, existing in different forms in different historical periods. Her book, *The New Jim Crow*, uses history to compare and contrast slavery, Jim Crow segregation, and what she calls the New Jim Crow, the mass incarceration of poor African American males, as different forms of racialized social control (Alexander 2012, 16–17).

Culture

In *Introduction to Sociology*, Basirico, Cashion and Eshleman (2014) defines culture as "a system of ideas, values, beliefs, knowledge, norms, customs and technology shared by almost everybody in a particular society" (97). Ritzer defines culture as "the ideas, values, practices and material objects that allow a group, people, even an entire society, to carry out their collective lives in relative order and harmony" (2015, 109). Giddens, Duneier, Appplebaum and Carr (2013, 43) define culture as "the values held by members of a particular group, the languages they speak, the symbols they revere, the norms they follow, and the material goods they create, from tools to clothing."

Conceptually, culture comes in many forms. There is ideal culture and real culture; symbolic conceptions of culture and material conceptions of culture; high and low culture, popular culture, folk culture; subcultures, counter cultures, culture wars, global culture, consumer culture, post-consumer culture, cyber culture, the culture of poverty, culture shock, the web of culture, cultural lag, cultural appropriation, and civic culture.

What this variety of definitions and forms of culture reveals is the variety of contexts in which the term culture can be used and the variety of meanings it can take on, depending on the purpose the user has set for it. What culture means is, in important ways, determined by who is using the term and what they are attempting to do with it.

Culture can be used in one context to refer to the physical objects that people construct and the "meaning" of those objects for those who view and use them. In another context, it can refer to the ideas, ways of thinking and speaking that people employ when they are trying to make sense of the social reality they share with those around them.

The best way to learn the meaning of culture is to look at how analysts use the term when they are trying to make sense of the social reality they are studying. In *Coming Apart*, Murray uses the term "civic culture" to describe the shared values, norms, beliefs, and activities that he argues were characteristic of "the American way of life" in the United States at his zero point of November 3, 1963. On that date, he argues, Americans shared the same culture because they watched the same television programs, went to see the same movies, drove the same kinds of cars, listened to the same music, ate the same kinds of foods, and read the same kinds of books (Murray 2012, 7). Most Americans in 1963, Murray argues, also shared the same beliefs about what people ought to do and how they ought to do it. In sociological terms, they agreed on what **statuses** people should occupy and what **roles** they should perform when they occupied those statuses. Almost all American adults got married. Murray argues that it was normal in 1963 for women, when they reached adulthood, to take on the status of wife and mother and to perform the role of homemaker and caregiver. Women who deviated from their proper status and role and got pregnant outside of marriage were "supposed" to either marry the father of their child or give the child up for adoption. It was normal for adult men to take on the status of husband and father and to perform the role of breadwinner for their family by joining the paid workforce.

Murray also argues that religiosity was a central aspect of American culture in 1963. Only 1 percent of respondents to a Gallup Poll question said they had no religious preference; half of all respondents said they had to been to church at least once in the past seven days. Almost all Americans (95%) defined themselves as working- or middle-class (Murray 2012, 8–9). Murray's point is not that the United States didn't have classes in 1963, but that people in different classes shared the same civic culture. His book is about how that shared civic culture has come apart.

Culture, or rather cultures, is also central to Kovach's *Indigenous Methodologies*. The problem she attempts to address is how and if two different cultures can be made commensurable. For her and people in her position, the problem is a critical and a personal one. She lives in two cultures: one indigenous, the other Western colonial. Her study is not historical but it deals with the effects of history. Western culture and indigenous cultures are not just different and separate; historically, the one has dominated and marginalized the other. Kovach is admittedly conflicted. By lineage she is Plains Cree and Salteaux. Her adoptive parents were eastern Europeans of Hungarian descent. "Both spoke the language. I was raised knowing that culture counts" (Kovach 2009, 4).

Kovach works in a Canadian university—in her terms, a colonial site. The problem she and others who share her position address is how and if it is possible to come to understand indigenous cultures in their own terms, using their own methodologies, in a manner acceptable to scholars in Western universities. "We know what we know from where we stand. We need to be honest about that. I situate myself not as a knowledge-keeper—this has not been my path—rather my role is facilitator. I have a responsibility to help create entry points for Indigenous knowledges to come through" (7).

Society and Social Stratification: Class, Caste, Gender, and Race

"Society" is to sociology what "culture" is to anthropology. Almost everybody uses the term and almost everybody uses it differently. Ritzer says that, traditionally, sociologists have "defined society as a complex pattern of social relationships that is bounded in space and persists in time" (2015, 195). He admits that the definition is very abstract and that, as a result, almost any social relationship, from a three-person triad to a nation state to the International Monetary Fund, could be viewed as a society. Giddens' (2013) definition is equally vague. "A society is a system of interrelationships that connects individuals together" (45).

Societies seem to almost inevitably be hierarchically organized; their members are rank ordered into unequal groups on the basis of attributes. Basirico, Cashion and Ross and Ritzer (2015) say that modern societies are stratified primarily on the basis of wealth, power, prestige, and social honor (Basirico, 234; Ritzer 2015, 253). Giddens (2013, 201) points out that those social rankings are also sometimes based on characteristics like gender and ethnicity.

Class and Caste

According to most sociology texts, modern societies are stratified mainly by **class**. Brian Obach (2014, 153) says the term class is used to "to refer to someone's position in the economy." A person's class position is determined by the quantity of wealth and income he or she possesses. Ritzer (2015, 253) says that "[t]hose who rank close to one another in wealth and income can be said to be members of the same social class." In addition to wealth and income, social class is often determined by **socioeconomic status** (SES), a combination of education, occupation, status, and prestige (Basirico, Cashion and Eshleman, 237). Ritzer distinguishes class systems of stratification from systems based on **caste** on the basis of key characteristics: class systems are more fluid; class position is in part achieved; class is economically based, large scale, and impersonal (2015, 203).

In sociology texts, caste systems are described as closed systems. In a caste system one's social status is given for life. "Everyone's social status is based on personal characteristics—such as perceived race or ethnicity ... parental religion or parental caste" Giddens (2013, 202). Giddens says that "caste societies" can be seen as a special type of class society—in which class position is ascribed at birth, rather than achieved through personal accomplishment. Caste systems, he adds, are maintained by systems of endogamy—marriage within one's caste is required by custom and law (202). Ritzer agrees that caste systems are rigid and closed (2015, 273).

RACE, SEX, AND GENDER

In introductory sociology texts, **race** is said to be socially defined on the basis of some real or presumed physical, biological characteristic of a person (Ritzer 2015, 293). Giddens, Duneier, Applebaum and Carr (2013, 298) say that race is "a classification system that assigns individuals and groups to categories that is ranked or hierarchical."

In sociology texts, **sex** is distinguished from **gender**. Sex is biological, determined at conception at the chromosomal level, manifesting itself in terms of primary sex characteristics. Gender is socially determined. The roles females and males perform, the behavioral differences between males and females, the differing treatment of males and females is, according to the texts, a matter of gender, not sex. If men are more aggressive and instrumental and women more nurturing and affective, this is more a matter of gender socialization than biology. "Sex refers to physical differences of the body, whereas gender concerns psychological, social and cultural differences between male and females. The distinction is fundamental, because many differences between males and females are not biological in origin" (Giddens, Duneier, Applebaum and Carr 2013, 265). Ritzer's distinction between sex and gender is slightly more nuanced. He says that "sex is 'principally' or 'mainly' a biological distinction" while gender is based on physical as well as behavioral characteristics "that are considered appropriate for each sex" (2015, 323).

When texts provide definitions of theoretical concepts, it can seem as if these concepts are part of social reality itself. It is important to remember, however, that these **concepts are analytical tools, not things. History, culture, society, class, caste, race, and gender aren't descriptions of reality. They are theoretical concepts that social analysts employ to make sense of social life and to construct their pictures of the social reality they study.**

COMBING CONCEPTS TO MAKE BETTER SENSE OF SOCIAL REALITY

For concepts like class, caste, race, ethnicity, and gender to help us make sense of social life, we often have to combine them. It doesn't make sense to view people exclusively as male or female, upper-class or lower-class, Latino, white or African American. They are white, male, and working class; female, upper-middle-class, and black; indigenous, poor, and female; German, British, or Canadian. Sometimes we not only have to combine our concepts to make sense of reality, we have to alter their meaning as well.

WOMEN AS A CONCEPT

Theoretical concepts can sometimes hide as much as they reveal. In *The XX Factor*, Wolf argues that "women" as a theoretical concept is no longer a terribly useful tool for making sense of contemporary life in developed societies; that although "[t]hrough most of human history it made sense to talk about 'women' en masse, today, it rarely does" (2013, x). She argues that women no longer behave similarly enough to use the same concept to make sense of all of them, because "they are different from each other, not just in their careers, family patterns and daily tasks, but even in the bedroom" (xiv).

CLASS

Charles Murray uses class to make sense of how he thinks the United States is coming apart. To do this he doesn't take an existing definition of class and apply it. Instead, he constructs two new social classes—a new upper class and a new lower class.

The concept of class is not as transparent as it may appear. Sociology texts tell us that social classes are distinguished from one another, at least in part, by differing levels of income and wealth. What they don't tell us is what level of income and wealth should be used to distinguish one class from another. What level of wealth and income constitutes an upper class—people in the top 20 percent; the top 10 percent; the top 1 percent? In practice this depends on what the classifier is trying to do with the concept. In *Coming Apart*, Murray constructs his new upper class out of Americans who rank in the top 5 percent in wealth and income. "The top five centile are important for our purposes because they contain almost all of the new upper class" (2012, 50). In addition to level of wealth and income, Murray uses occupation to construct his new upper class. "I have used the top 5 percent of people in managerial occupations and the professions as a working definition of the new upper class" (52). For Murray, class is as much a matter of lifestyle as income and wealth. It is high levels of wealth and income that enable people in managerial and professional positions to develop a lifestyle through which they distinguish and separate themselves from everybody else. It is this lifestyle, this distinction and separation, which is essential to his account of why the United States is coming apart.

Murray constructs his new lower class out of four components. He includes people between 20 and 49 years of age who rank in the bottom 30 percent of wealth and income. Out of this age grouping he only includes healthy men who are "not bringing home enough income to put themselves and one other adult above the poverty line" (227). He also includes single women with children, and men and women who are "disconnected from the matrix of community life—people who belong to no organizations at all" (229). This may be a quixotic way of constructing a class, but it serves his purposes. When analysts use the term class it's important to keep in mind what they mean by it, how they use it, and for what purposes.

Caste

Alexander and Wolf construct a concept of caste to fit their own purposes. Neither uses caste as a form of society. They see modern societies as stratified by both caste and class. Alexander combines concepts of race and caste to make sense of the situation of African Americans in the United States throughout its history. She uses the term "racial caste ... to denote a stigmatized racial group locked into an inferior position by law and custom. Jim Crow and slavery were caste systems. So is our current system of mass incarceration" (Alexander 2012, 12). Though Alexander uses racial caste to make sense of the condition of African Americans, she doesn't place all African Americans inside her racial caste. There were African Americans who were not slaves; there were African Americans who were not subjected to Jim Crow laws, and there are African Americans who are not subject to the regime of mass incarceration.

Wolf combines the concepts of gender and caste to make sense of the condition of women throughout most of human history. She says that until forty years ago, the lives of women could be understood in terms of their gender. Their position was determined by the ascribed characteristics of gender and maintained by law and custom. Their life chances were defined by whom and if they married. If they worked, they worked at jobs restricted to those who shared their gender. When they married, they left the workforce for housekeeping and child-rearing. While Alexander employs the concept of racial caste to make sense of the condition of African Americans throughout the history of the United States, Wolf uses the concept of gender caste to make sense of that group of well-educated professional women in developed societies who over the last forty years have escaped it.

Conclusion

Introductory texts provide broad definitions of a great many theoretical concepts—so many that just getting the definitions straight and distinguishing one from another is a challenge. This approach has its merits. After all, you have to start somewhere.

In practice, however, the meaning of these concepts is determined by their use. I have tried to emphasize that **theoretical concepts are tools, not things**. Social analysts use them to construct the pictures of social reality which they in turn use to address the social and intellectual problems they have set for themselves.

Just as concepts are tools, not things, so data is constructed, not discovered. In methods classes, we learn to master techniques (qualitative and quantitative) for constructing data. These techniques are only part of what we mean by methods, however. Methods are also particular approaches to the study of social life. Variants of what is called the scientific method is one such approach, the interpretive another. Kovach will introduce a very different approach, which she calls indigenous methodology.

Study Questions

1. How do Murray, Alexander, and Wolf use their particular conception of history in their studies?
2. Select one concept—culture, caste, class, or gender—and compare how it is defined in Wikipedia with how it is used by Murray, Alexander, Wolf, or Kovach.
3. How and in what sense are theoretical concepts tools rather than things?
4. What do I mean when I say that Murray creates two new classes in *Coming Apart*?
5. How does Alexander combine the concept of caste and race? How does she use the combined concept she creates in *The New Jim Crow*?
6. How does Wolf combine the concept of gender and caste? How does she use this combined concept in *The XX Factor*?

Assignments

1. Identify some of the major theoretical concepts employed in the reading(s) you have selected. Look up these concepts in *Wikipedia*. How does the use of these concepts by the author of your selected reading differ from the *Wikipedia* definitions?
2. Make an educated guess as why you think the problem that you plan to address in your research project proposal exists. Think of your educated guess as a hypothesis and describe it in a paragraph or two.

Suggested Further Readings

Bourdieu, Pierre. 1984. *Distinction*, xi–7 (Preface to the English Edition and Introduction).

Foucault, Michel. 1965. *Madness and Civilization*, ix–xii (Preface). Translated by Richard Howard. New York: New American Library.

Rosanvallon, Pierre. 2007. "Intellectual History and Democracy: An Interview with Pierre Rosanvallon." *Journal of the History of Ideas* 68, 703–715.

CHAPTER 4

USING METHODS AS TOOLS

What we today call the social sciences have been developing for over a century. Over this time, the methodological techniques for creating data and the ways social scientists employ the data they create have become routine and are often unquestioned by those who use them. Because "current approaches to the relation between theory, methods and observations often sap the joy from social research" (Tavory and Timmermans 2014, 7) it is important reexamine these techniques and how we use them. Social science should be a process of creating new conjectures about the world. It should be about stimulating insights, producing surprises, and rethinking what we think we know about the social world. Remember, one of the first maxims of sociology is that things aren't what they seem. The research process should result in new insights into our lives and new and different ways of coming to understand important social problems. If it doesn't do that then it isn't worth doing.

The founders of sociology developed new ways of conceiving of and studying social life. They created new concepts, designed new methods for studying the social world, and developed new methodological techniques for constructing data to develop and test surprising and interesting hypotheses about the modern world. It is worth briefly reviewing what they did and how they did it before looking at how contemporary thinkers use their tools to theorize about the world in which we live, and how you might use concepts, methods, and data to do your own theorizing.

Social Science and the Scientific Method

The fundamental ways (most) sociologists study contemporary society were established by Emile Durkheim and Max Weber at the beginning of the twentieth century. In the back of their minds when they did so was the specter of Karl Marx, whose approach to the study of modern society had become the inspiration for radical working-class movements throughout Europe. Both Weber and Durkheim were interested in developing an approach to the study of human social life that could provide a scientific alternative to Marx's historical materialism.

DURKHEIMIAN SOCIOLOGY

Durkheim conceived of sociology as a science of morality. When we study value and norms, normality and deviance, we are studying the societal basis of the moral systems that govern us. Durkheim believed that the societal basis of these moral systems could be studied scientifically. The reason introductory sociology texts begin their methods sections with an account of the scientific method is because most (though certainly not all) social scientists conceive of science as a method. Many social scientists believe that all sciences employ the same methods and procedures, they just use them to study different things—biologists, biological organisms; sociologists, societies. Durkheim believed that for sociology to be a science, it had to carve out an area of nature peculiar to it and then employ the scientific method to the study of that area. He tried to establish the scientific status of sociology by identifying the existence of social facts, facts that could not be reduced either to human biology or individual psychology. Social facts, he argued, are forces external to individual human beings that drive them to behave in particular ways. These moral forces are what we would now call values and norms. We recognize their existence most acutely when we try to act in opposition to them. Durkheim argued that these forces did not originate in biology or the individual psyche. They originated in society. Durkheim conceived of sociology as the application of the scientific method to study these social facts and the societies that gave rise to them. Many contemporary sociologists have followed his lead.

Social Facts

"a category of facts with very distinctive characteristics: it consists of ways of acting, thinking and feeling, external to the individual, and endowed with the power of coercion, by reason of which they control him."

Figure 4.1: Social Facts

DURKHEIM'S METHOD

While he believed that the study of society could not be reduced to biology, Durkheim also believed that variants of the same methods and procedures biologists employed to study biological organisms could be applied to the study of society. Accordingly,

Durkheim developed a taxonomy of societies. This taxonomy classified all societies on the basis of the way they were structured and how that structure enabled that society to fulfill the functions necessary to keep it in a healthy state. Simple, or in his terms segmented societies, are tied together mechanically in the sense that all the parts (clans made up of families and extended families) are pretty much the same. The social division of labor between the parts is very simple. The only thing that really ties such societies together is a shared moral order embodied in religion which, Durkheim argued, is society worshipping itself.

More complex social organisms, the ones Durkheim was really interested in studying, were characterized by an increasingly elaborate division of labor, which he called organic. In this type of society, each part is differentiated from and connected to the others, like the organs of the human body. The parts or organs of society work in tandem to keep it in a healthy state. The very interdependence of the parts of modern societies require people living in them to perform increasingly specialized tasks. This very specialization makes people dependent on one another. No one in a complex modern society is capable of going it alone.

Durkheim insisted that this increasingly intricate division of labor subjected such societies to a particular form of illness or pathology that he called an anomie. In his time, the most dangerous form of anomie was class conflict. When business owners and their workers fought against each other, instead of cooperating for the benefit of society as a whole, that was a symptom of anomie. Durkheim maintained that class conflict is not inherent to modern society (as Marx did), but rather a form of pathology that can be avoided or overcome.

One of the major responsibilities of sociologists, Durkheim argued, is to determine whether the society they study is in a normal or an anomic state, and whether the social facts whose effects they observe are normal or pathological. Contemporary sociologists no longer conceive of society as an organism, but they do study society's social structure (how the parts of society fit together), and many classify societies by kind—developed, developing, underdeveloped, modern, postmodern, premodern. Many also believe in the evolutionary development of one kind of society into another—underdeveloped and premodern societies develop into developed modern societies and are still developing into postindustrial, postmodern societies. Some sociologists refer to this process as modernization.

DURKHEIM'S SURPRISES: CRIME AND SUICIDE

Part of Durkheim's greatness was his ability to employ his way of studying society to come up with surprising possibilities. Most strikingly, he argued that crime and suicide are not what they seem. On the face of it, crime would appear to be patho-logical. After all, while what constitutes criminal behavior differs from society to society, every society condemns it and attempts to stamp it out. Indeed, Durkheim defined crime as behavior that brings forth punitive sanctions. Yet this, Durkheim argued, is precisely what makes the existence of crime normal. If crime is a social universal, he reasoned, it must perform some positive function. What might the positive functions of crime be? He suggested three possible social functions of crime. Firstly, crime strengthens the very moral and legal order it violates, by increasing the widespread adherence of people to that order in their abhorrence of the crime and the criminal. Secondly, the punishment of crime and the criminal increases people's confidence in the strength of the moral and legal order. Finally, some crime might actually contribute to positive changes in the moral and legal order. After all, Durkheim reasoned, if there was no crime, the moral and legal order of a society would never change or develop, and it needs to change and develop. For that to happen, some of what is judged criminal at one time has to become normal at another time. Yesterday's drug kingpin is today a perfectly respectable Colorado business person (1964, 65–73). While Durkheim argued that the existence of crime is normal, whether the society in which crime occurs is in a normal or pathological state is determined by the rate at which crime occurs and the popular reaction to criminality (1964, 66).

As with crime, Durkheim argued that suicide is not what it appears to be. Durkheim didn't contest that individuals took their own lives for a variety of per-sonal reasons. He did, however, develop a system of kinds of reasons for committing suicide: altruistic, anomic, egoistic, and fatalistic. He argued that which of these reasons are most prevalent and whether suicide rates went up or down are the result of the kind of society in which suicide takes place, the position those who commit suicide occupy in society, and the state of that society when suicide occurs. The point I want to make here is not whether Durkheim's hypotheses about crime and suicide were right or wrong. My point is rather that Durkheim used his way of conceiving of and studying social life to develop hypothetical explanations of social phenomena that were counterintuitive, intriguing, and surprising. In other words, he used his sociological method to investigate whether things were the way they seemed.

WEBERIAN SOCIOLOGY

Max Weber's sociology, like Durkheim's, originated in part as a debate with Marx and his followers. It was also an attempt to provide an answer to those who argued that human social life could not be studied with the methods and procedures employed in the natural sciences, because human beings were not governed by natural laws but by reasons, motives, and persons. There were those then (and still are those now) who argued that the way people think about and experience social life differs from society to society and time period to time period. If you want to understand why people do what they do, they argue, you have to understand the way the people you study think, reason, and experience the social world. People living in different societies at different times think about and experience the world differently (Radkau 2011, 252). This way of viewing social life is no longer dominant among sociologists, but still has a significant number of adherents. Just because most sociologists don't study social life in these terms doesn't mean those who do are wrong.

Instead of starting with social wholes (societies) as Durkheim did, Weber started with what he called human social action. He defined social action as meaningful behavior directed at another. The key to understanding social action and interaction, Weber argued, is to understand what the people involved in this action were trying to achieve through it. To do so, he developed a way of conceptualizing different forms of rationality. Instrumental rationality is the use of reason to attempt to achieve ends in the most efficient way possible. Value rationality is the use of reason to attempt to act in accordance with moral ends. Traditional rationality is the use of reason in an attempt to act in accordance with established ways of doing things. He called behavior that was an expression of an emotional state emotional rationality, though of course behavior so motivated isn't really rational at all. Weber argued that his way of categorizing forms of rationality made it possible to study human motivations scientifically. Sociologists could observe social action and interaction to infer which form of rationality governed human behavior, and thereby uncover the meaning that lay behind it. Categorizing forms of rationality in this way also made it possible to determine which form of rationality was dominant in a society at any given point in time. Weber argued that modern societies are increasingly dominated by instrumental rationality.

Weber's Surprise: Religion and the Rise of Capitalism

Weber's most famous hypothesis was developed in contradistinction to what he took to be the Marxist conception of the relationship between thinking and economic conditions. Marx ([1856] 1970, 21) famously argued that "it is not the consciousness of men that determines their existence, but their social existence that determines their consciousness." Put more simply, he argued that the way people think is a product of the way they live. Weber argued that this way of viewing the relationship between the way we think and the kind of society in which we live is too simple and unidirectional. He argued instead that ideas play an important role in the development of ways of life and kinds of society, including capitalism. Like Durkheim, Weber employed his sociological method to develop a surprising hypothetical answer to an important social and historical question: why did capitalism develop first in northern Europe in the sixteenth century?

At its beginnings, Weber ([1904] 2009, 83) argued, capitalism requires the most irrational of behaviors: hard work in pursuit of material gain, which instead of being spent on the satisfaction of personal wants and desires, is saved and reinvested. What could possibly motivate anyone to behave in such a fashion? Weber's hypothesis was that Calvinism provided such a motive. Calvinists, he argued, worked hard at their calling (what God had called them to do) not for material gain, but to serve God. If their work was blessed with success and they lived a sober and industrious style of life, that might be a sign (though an uncertain one) that they were amongst the Elect, those few who God had (for His own reasons), decided to save rather than damn. Thus, at its beginnings, the capitalist spirit was a largely unintended consequence of a religious ethic.

To test this hypothesis (that Protestantism was a causal factor in the rise of capitalism), Weber used what is today called the historical comparative method. He studied the ethical orientation promoted by different religions in different world areas. He concluded that a number of these areas possessed many of the preconditions necessary for the development of capitalism. It was primarily the ethical orientation promoted by their dominant religions that held them back. He argued that Protestantism embodied a particular ethical orientation toward life that was a necessary though not sufficient condition for the birth of capitalism. It was not enough on its own to bring about the birth of capitalism. Other factors were crucial as well—Roman and Church law, the relative autonomy of cities, double-entry bookkeeping, the growth of an independent civil service—but without the Protestant ethic, capitalism wouldn't have developed when and where it did.

Social Action

"We shall speak of 'action' in so far as the acting individual attaches a subjective meaning to his behavior ... Action is 'social' insofar as its subjective meaning takes account of the behavior of others and is thereby oriented in its course."

Max Weber, *Economy and Society*, p. 4

Figure 4.2: Social Action

The Protestant Ethic and the Spirit of Capitalism

"...one of the constutive components of the modern campitalist spirit and, moreover, generally of modern civilization, was the rational organization of life on the basis of the idea of calling. It was born out of the spirit of Christian asceticism."

Max Weber, *The Protestant Ethic and the Spirit of Capitalism*

Figure 4.3: Protestant Ethic and the Spirit of Capitalism

Weber's application of the historical comparative method to the study of world religions led him to the conclusion that the Protestant ethic was a crucial part of a more general, long-term process in Europe that led to the increasing dominance of instrumental rationality over traditional and value rationality. The ethical orientation embodied in the dominant religions in other world areas impeded the development of instrumental rationality in those areas (Weber [1905] 1972, 205–16). Again, my point here is not that Weber's hypothesis about the causal import of Protestantism in the birth of capitalism is correct (that is still hotly debated amongst social scientists—see Swatos and Kaelber 2005). It is rather that Weber employed his historical comparative method to develop and test a fascinating and intriguing hypothetical answer to a very important question.

METHODS AS TECHNIQUES FOR CREATING DATA

The major approaches to the scientific study of sociology originated with Durkheim and Weber. Each used this approach (they are two variants of essentially the same approach) and their sociological imaginations to generate counterintuitive, surprising, and intriguing hypotheses to address significant social questions and problems. The data they created and employed to sustain these hypotheses are primitive by contemporary standards. During the last half century, techniques for creating data, particularly quantitative techniques, have advanced much more quickly than has theorizing. We usually don't think of data as being created, but it is. That isn't to say it is made up or false. Whether data is reliable or not is a product of how well it is made, not if it is made. The process of mastering the use of various methodological techniques for creating data is so challenging that we often forget what we use these techniques for.

You should begin your evaluation of the theorizing that underlies a social study by asking if the problem the study addresses is significant, and if its conclusions are in any way surprising or interesting. Then, you need to identify the tools (concepts, methods, and data) employed to address the problem the study addresses and evaluate if they are the best tools employed in the best way to address that problem. Let's look at the methods and techniques employed by the authors of the studies we will analyze in upcoming chapters to demonstrate how this might be done.

MURRAY'S USE OF DATA IN COMING APART

Though he doesn't say so explicitly, Charles Murray employs Durkheim's approach to the study of social life in *Coming Apart*. He argues that contemporary American society is in an anomic or pathological state. To make his argument, he identifies an historical point at which America was in a healthy condition, with a shared culture and widespread belief in a shared value and norm system. He then tries to show that, over the last half century, that common culture and shared value and norm system have come apart.

Murray argues that there was a shared civic culture in the United States in the early 1960s. To do so, he uses databases available online—the Current Population Survey, The Motion Picture Association of America Production Code website, the Roper public opinion research website, and the FBI website. There is nothing wrong with this. There is no sense creating data that is already there to be used. When you use existing databases, however, it is important to realize that this data was often created for other purposes. Roper rates television programs to help networks decide which shows to continue and which ones to drop. The Motion Picture Association created a code with which to rate movies to make sure parents knew which films their kids should watch, which ones they shouldn't, and which kinds of movies shouldn't be produced or shown at all. As a result, this data doesn't always fit Murray's purpose. For instance, the Current Population Survey in 1963 didn't ask if married women working outside the house had children or not. It did a few years later, so he used that data, assuming that what was true then was probably true in earlier years as well.

Murray argues that by 2010 America's shared culture and value and norm system had come apart, and that America is in an anomic state. He argues that a new upper and lower class has developed, each with very different values and norms. To substantiate this, Murray begins with Census tract data, Department of Labor statistics, and reports from elite colleges and universities on their alumni. He then uses these sources to create new data to fit his needs. By applying some fairly sophisticated statistical techniques to the existing data, he is able to differentiate population clusters by location, education, profession, and income. His conceptualization of class, culture, and subcultures, and the data he employs and creates are all parts of the picture he draws of social life at two points in time: tied together normally in the early 1960s, coming apart pathologically by 2010.

ALEXANDER'S USE OF DATA IN *THE NEW JIM CROW*

In *The New Jim Crow*, Alexander conceives of crime and punishment as social facts. Unlike Durkheim, Alexander thinks these social facts were consciously created. She tries to demonstrate that crime rates are constructed by changes in criminal statutes, the interpretation of those statues by courts, and police policies and tactics.

The Fourth Amendment

The right of the people to be secure in their persons, houses, papers, and effects, against unreasonable searches and seizures, shall not be violated, and no Warrants shall issue, but upon probable cause, supported by Oath or affirmation, and particularly describing the place to be searched, and the persons or things to be seized.

Figure 4.4: The Fourth Amendment

The Fourth Amendment to the US Constitution was passed to prevent government agents from unwarranted search and seizure of our person and our property. What that means in practice is determined by court rulings in cases in which the defendant argues that their Fourth Amendment rights have been violated. Alexander uses Supreme Court decisions (*Terry v. Ohio, Florida v. Bostick, Schneckloth v. Bustamonte, Ohio v. Robinette, Atwater v. City of Lago Vista*) in such cases to argue that the War on Drugs made virtually all police searches "reasonable."

As she points out, increasing police power to search people for drugs doesn't in itself explain why police use this power. As part of the War on Drugs, the federal government provided substantial economic incentives to state and local police to exercise this power. These incentives provided instrumental reasons for police and police departments to vastly increase the number of such drug searches. The Edward Byrne Memorial State and Local Enforcement Assistance Program, the Drug Enforcement Administration, and the Military Cooperation with Civilian Law Enforcement Agencies Act offered federal money, equipment, and training to state and local police departments who participated in the War on Drugs.

The Comprehensive Drug Abuse Prevention and Control Act allowed police to seize any property or cash which they had "probable cause" to believe was involved in drug trafficking. As a result of these incentives, drug arrests skyrocketed. The Anti-Drug Abuse Act established long mandatory prison sentences for drug offenses. This gave people charged with drug offenses strong incentives (instrumental reasons) to accept plea bargains and plead guilty in order to receive shorter sentences than they might have gotten had they gone to trial. The result has been a vast increase in the number of people incarcerated in our prisons. Alexander uses objective evidence available to anyone who wishes to look for it (LexisNexis is an excellent way to access court decisions and articles in law journals) to support her hypothesis that the increase in crime and incarceration rates is the result of federal policy. Just as Weber argued that a religious ethic may have been necessary for the onset of capitalism, but was no longer necessary once capitalism had been established, Alexander argues that the incentives provided by the federal government to local and state police to participate in the War on Drugs are no longer necessary now that the War on Drugs war has been institutionalized. Now that it is established, the War on Drugs is business as usual for state and local police departments.

Alison Wolf's Creation and Use of Data in *The XX Factor*

Weber argued that the birth of capitalism was in part an unintended consequence of religious Calvinists' attempt to look for signs of whether or not they were amongst the Saved. Alison Wolf hypothesizes that growing inequality and the separation of one group of women from others is an unintended consequence of the rise of well-educated, well-paid professional women. These women didn't intend to achieve these results. They just wanted to make a better life for themselves.

The rise of this new group of women, Wolf argues, is the result of millions of individual decisions made largely on the basis of instrumental rationality. Like Weber, Wolf argues that these women's actions were meaningful. They used instrumental reasons in an effort to improve their lives. Like Durkheim, Wolf argues that millions of individual decisions resulted in similar social changes in all developed societies, because these societies are structured in similar ways. Millions of women trying to advance their individual ends caused social changes that few, if any of them, either intended or were aware of. As a result, 15 to 20 percent of women advanced in ways women had never advanced before. The other 80 to 85 percent, using the same kind of instrumental reasoning, continued to live lives as women always have.

As is the case with Murray, the data Wolf uses to substantiate her hypothesis is taken largely from existing databases. Just because Wolf and Murray didn't create the data they use doesn't mean it wasn't created. They didn't create or administer the surveys, construct the samples, or collect and deposit the results, but somebody did. Without this data, Murray's and Wolf's books would be just speculation. Wolf, Murray, and Alexander employ historical methods to address the problem their studies address. They, like us, have access to a great deal of data not available to Durkheim and Weber to make their cases. "In the half century since 1970 human societies have studied and measured themselves as never before in history. ... Statistical data, high speed computing and academic publishing have produced a flood of empirical studies" (Wolf 2013, xiii).

Because Wolf is arguing that the social changes she describes have occurred in pretty much the same way in all developed countries, the databases she employs are different than those used by Murray. Governments in developed countries create and collect the same kinds of data as the United States does, and for many of the same reasons. In addition, these countries as a group and the United Nations also create, collect, and archive data. This data is available online.

THE SEARCH FOR INCONVENIENT FACTS

Wolf doesn't just employ these databases to confirm her hypothesis. She actively looks for data which would throw her hypothesis into question. It is possible to argue, contrary to Wolf, that the changes in women's lives that have occurred in developed societies are the result of deliberate government policies favoring gender equality. If they were, Wolf reasons, Sweden and the Netherlands, whose governments have pursued such policies much more consistently than has the United States, should look much different. The data, she says, indicates that they don't. The same separation between the top 15 percent of women and the rest of women exists in all developed countries. Why? Women faced with different opportunities using instrumental reason to improve their lives produced similar results in all developed countries. Conscious government policy seems to have had little effect on this process.

Inconvenient Facts

"The primary task of a useful teacher is to teach his students to recognize 'inconvenient' facts—I mean facts that are inconvenient for their party [political] opinions. And for every party opinion there are facts that are extremely inconvenient, for my own opinion no less than for others. I believe the teacher accomplishes more than a mere intellectual task if he compels his audience to accustom itself to the existence of such facts. I would be so immodest as even to apply the expression 'moral achievement,' though perhaps this may sound too grandiose for something that should go without saying."

Max Weber, *Science as a Vocation*

Figure 4.5: Inconvenient Facts

INDIGENOUS METHODOLOGIES

In *Indigenous Methodologies*, Margaret Kovach shows how to use indigenous methods to study indigenous communities. Indigenous methods are first of all experiential. They require the researcher to examine their own life experiences as part of their preparation for studying indigenous communities. The methods she suggests are quite similar to those Weber rejected. Indigenous knowledge takes the form of an understanding of the unique ways in which indigenous communities understand and experience their world. To gain an understanding of this understanding, to make sense of the sense they make of their world, the researcher must embrace that world and participate in it. Central to this social world is the belief that all the generations that make up a people remain part of that people. The spirit of a people's ancestors remains alive and present even after they have died. The community's knowledge of itself is passed down from generation to generation in the form of stories. There are different kinds of stories—creation stories, teaching stories, and personal narratives of place, happenings, and experiences. Understanding these stories and telling one's own stories in talking circles is key to the indigenous method of research.

CONCLUSION

As I hope this chapter has made clear, "method" refers both to the particular ways social scientists approach the study of social life and to the techniques they use to create data. Along with concepts, methods and data are the tools and raw materials social analysts employ to paint their pictures of social life. By designing these pictures, they try to demonstrate how and why the social problems their studies address exist.

In the following six chapters I will provide examples of how to uncover, describe, and evaluate the theorizing that underlies social studies. When you read these chapters, keep in mind that these examples are provided to show you how to analyze and evaluate the theorizing underlying social studies on your own. To get the most out of these examples, you should be analyzing similar studies as you read these chapters. You should also be designing a research project proposal in which you describe how you would do your own theorizing on a topic and question of your own choosing. The assignments at the end of each chapter are designed to provide you with a step-by-step guide to help you do both.

GOOD DATABASES AND HOW TO FIND THEM ONLINE

Court cases and law journal articles in the United States, the United Kingdom, and Australia

www.lexisnexis.com/en-us/home.page
https://www.lexisnexis.com/uk/legal/
https://www.lexisnexis.com/au/legal

US Census Bureau statistics

http://factfinder2.census.gov/faces/nav/jsf/pages/index.xhtml

Canadians statistics, kept by Statistics Canada

http://www.statcan.gc.ca/start-debut-eng.html

United Kingdom statistics

https://www.cia.gov/library/publications/the-world-factbook/

Global databases

International Labor Organization
http://www.ilo.org/global/statistics-and-databases/lang--en/index.htm

United Nations Educational Scientific and Cultural Organization (UNESCO)
http://www.uis.unesco.org/Pages/default.aspx

World Health Organization
http://www.who.int/whosis/en/

World Bank
http://data.worldbank.org/

International Monetary Fund
http://www.imf.org/external/data.htm

Organization for Economic Cooperation and Development
http://www.oecd.org/statistics/

STUDY QUESTIONS

1. What is the scientific method?
2. How did Durkheim use the scientific method to study social life?
3. What method did Weber use to study world religions?
4. What did Durkheim mean by social facts?
5. Why did Durkheim consider crime to be normal?
6. Why did Durkheim think that suicide was social in nature?
7. What did Weber mean by social action?
8. How did Weber differentiate between different kinds of rationality?
9. What form of rationality did Weber think was dominant in the modern world?
10. Why did Weber think that Protestantism was a necessary condition to the emergence of capitalism in Europe?

Assignments

1. Describe some of the methodological approaches the author of the study you are analyzing employs to construct her picture of social reality.
2. What kinds of data does the author of your study use? Does she create her own data? Does she use databases, and if so, where does she find them?
3. Let's assume you have the chance to devote an entire semester to a research project addressing the problem and testing the hypothesis you described in previous assignments. To get the go-ahead to do the project, you have to submit a research project proposal to a professor who would sponsor your project. As part of that proposal, you have to describe your qualifications for being able to do the project. Describe those qualifications. Include relevant curiosities, concerns, and passions; life experiences; courses you have taken; reading you have done; and other research experience and tools you have in your description.

Suggested Further Readings

Durkheim, Emile. [1938] 1951. *Suicide*, edited by George Simpson, 145–52 (How to Determine Social Causes and Social Types). Translated by John A. Spaulding and George Simpson. New York: Free Press.

Durkheim, Emile. [1938] 1965. *Rules of Sociological Method*, edited by George E. G. Catlin, 1–13 (What Is a Social Fact). Translated by Sarah A. Solavay and John M. Mueller. New York: Free Press.

Weber, Max. *The Protestant Ethic and the Spirit of Capitalism*. 2009. New York: Oxford University Press 103–12 (Calvinism).

Weber, Max. 1978. *Economy and Society*, edited by Guenther Roth and Claus Wittich, 4–24 (The Definition of Sociology and of Social Action). Berkeley: University of California Press.

Image Credits

Fig. 4.2: Max Weber, "Social Action," Economy and Society. Copyright © 1978 by University of California Press.

Fig. 4.3: Max Weber, "Protestant Ethic and the Spirit of Capitalism," The Protestant Ethic and the Spirit of Capitalism. Copyright © 2009 by Wilder Publications.

Fig. 4.4: "The Fourth Amendment," The United States Constitution. Copyright in the Public Domain.

Fig. 4.5: Max Weber, "Inconvenient Facts," Science as a Vocation. Copyright in the Public Domain.

CHAPTER 5

CHARLES MURRAY'S *COMING APART: THE STATE OF WHITE AMERICA, 1960–2010*

LOOSENING CULTURAL CONNECTIONS, PART I: THE MAKING OF THE NEW UPPER CLASS

The authors of the studies we will examine begin, as I have suggested most social studies begin, with curiosity, concern, and passion. Curiosity, concern, and passion are directed at particular topics that are of interest to particular publics. The authors then employ their sociological imagination to transform their topic into a social or intellectual problem. They address this problem using theoretical concepts, methods, and data to design a pattern of connections amongst social phenomena that constitute a picture of social life. They argue that the social or intellectual problem they address exists because social life looks like and works the way the picture they have constructed indicates.

USING CURIOSITY, CONCERN, AND PASSION TO TRANSFORM A TOPIC INTO A PROBLEM

Our analysis of the theorizing that underlies *Coming Apart* begins with the identification of the curiosities, concerns, and passions of its author. Charles Murray is curious about the social effects of innate intellectual differences between people. In *The Bell Curve* (1994) he and Richard J. Herrnstein argued that intelligence is a better predictor of many social outcomes than is parental socioeconomic status or educational attainment. In this highly controversial book, he speculated that were we to eliminate discrimination by race, ethnicity, and gender, these intellectual differences would come to the fore and might be harder on those at the wrong end of the intellectual bell curve. In a social world in which some people are disadvantaged because of their race, ethnicity, or gender, They reasoned, they might justly blame their lot on the social injustices to which they are subjected. Remove these injustices, create a real meritocracy, and people would be more likely to blame themselves for their lack of success.

Murray is concerned about the social effects of government policies. In *Losing Ground* (1994) 1984, he argued that social democratic policies designed to aid the poor and disadvantaged often make their condition worse. Such programs, he argued, reward short-sighted behavior that makes it more difficult for the poor and disadvantaged to improve their situation in the long run.

Murray is a passionate libertarian and American nationalist. What makes the United States exceptional, in his view, is what he calls the American Project. He believes that, for most of its history, the United States has been dedicated to the proposition that human beings should be left free to live their lives as individuals and families as they think best. Left to their own devices, Americans came together voluntarily to solve the problems with which they were faced. Murray (2012, 308) argues "that the framework created by the American founders, stripped of its acceptance of slavery, is the best possible way to enable people of all kinds to pursue happiness."

Charles Murray is sixty-seven years old. He grew up in Newton, Iowa. He credits his high Scholastic Aptitude Test (SAT) scores with getting him out of small-town Iowa and into Harvard, where received a BA in history in 1965. He went on to get a PhD in political science from Massachusetts Institute of Technology in 1974. Since then he has worked for a number of right-leaning research institutes, and is currently the W. H. Brady Scholar at the American Enterprise Institute. In *Coming Apart*, Murray uses his sociological imagination to connect his own biographical situation with that of "other people like him." He does this by placing such people in the cognitive elite and the narrow and broad elites that run most American institutions. His picture of the United States, how it looks and works, places people like himself within a pattern of connections.

For Murray, social and economic inequality is not in itself a problem. The social problem the United States faces, in his view, is that social and economic inequality has laid the basis for the formation of two new social classes, which, because of their wide diversity of income and lifestyle, have grown increasingly separate from one another. The new upper class and the new lower class, in his view, live in separate worlds. The people who belong to these new classes not only don't care about each other, they are increasingly, as a practical matter, unaware of each other. Each class lives in its own bubble. This is a significant social problem, in Murray's view, because it rips asunder the shared civic culture that once held the United States together as a society. In Durkheim's terms, this has put the United States in an anomic condition.

Figure 5.1: President John F. Kennedy and First Lady Jacqueline Kennedy Arrive in Dallas

HISTORY AND CULTURE

In order to describe the social problem he has identified, Murray constructs two pictures of social life in the United States. The first picture is his portrait of the United States as it looked and worked in the early 1960s. This picture functions as his historical zero point, the latest point at which the social problem he wants to address did not yet exist. He selects November 22, 1963, the date President Kennedy was assassinated, as the symbolic marker of this zero point, the point at which one culture began to erode and two new subcultures began to develop in its place (Murray 2012, 1).

Murray employs the concept of civic culture to establish connections amongst the people living in the United States at his zero point (12). He argues that this shared culture—set of ideas, values, beliefs, norms, customs, and material objects shared by almost everybody in the United States in 1963—enabled them to carry out

Figure 5.2: Family Watching Television 1958

their collective lives in relative order and harmony. This civic culture, he argues, constituted a way of life for people living in the United States at this time.

Murray uses the concept of culture, along with polling and survey data, to establish a set of connections between the material objects Americans used, the mass media messages they received, the music they listened to, and the food they ate, along with their beliefs, values, and norms.

Americans were connected to one another culturally by the automobile. In 1963, most Americans drove cars made in America and, because there were only three American car manufacturers at the time, they drove pretty much the same kinds of cars.

He also connects Americans through common ownership of another material object, the television. In 1963, 93 percent of American families owned a television. Because there were only three commercial television networks at this time, Americans were connected by the television programs they watched. Murray uses Nielsen ratings to document Americans' television viewing habits. The television programs on offer validated and reinforced the same norms and values. "Whether television was portraying loving traditional families or pointing with alarm to the perils of violating the code, television was a team player. It was taken for granted that television programs were supposed to validate the standards that were commonly accepted as part of 'the American way of life'" (Murray 2012, 5).

Murray connects Americans by another leisure activity: going to the movies. The kinds of movies Americans could watch at this time were regulated by the Production Code of the Motion Picture Association of America. This code regulated the content of movies. Movie dialogue could couldn't contain profanity or swearing, ridicule religion, or make any but the most indirect suggestion of sexuality. Actors couldn't appear naked or even dance in a sexually suggestive manner (5).

Americans were connected by the music they listened to on the radio. Popular music consisted of a single Top 40 list, with rock, country, and a fair number of 1950s-style ballads lumped together. There were no separate stations specializing in different genres, except for country music channels in a few sections of the country (3). Murray connects Americans by the kinds of food they ate when they went to restaurants. Restaurants offered the same kinds of food. "In a large city, you would be able to find a few restaurants serving Americanized Chinese food, a few Italian restaurants serving spaghetti and pizza and a few restaurants with a French name" (3).

While the connections Murray established amongst Americans living in the early 1960s were a matter of shared tastes and preferences, at least some of these shared tastes and preferences were established in part by the limited options then available, and reinforced by regulatory bodies and codes that saw to it that any other possible options were closed off.

Murray also connects people through the use of quantitative evidence of their shared beliefs, values, and norms. He documents Americans' shared religiosity by citing the findings of a Gallup Poll taken in October 1963. When asked about their religious preference, only 1 percent of respondents answered "none." Half of the respondents answered that they had attended church at least once in the last week (Murray 2012, 6). Murray says that this shared religiosity didn't vary by class or level of educational attainment. "These answers showed almost no variation across classes. Poor or rich, high school dropout or college graduate, the percentage of Americans who said they were religious believers and had recently attended a worship service were close to identical" (6).

He uses the findings of the 1963 Current Population Survey to establish that Americans at this time were connected by shared beliefs about family and gender roles. According to the findings of this survey, only 3.5 percent of households were headed by a divorced person, and 1.6 percent by a separated person. Again, Murray reinforces the connection he has established by adding that "the marriage percentages for college grads and high school dropouts were about the same" (4). While the illegitimacy rate was "rising worrisomely amongst negroes," the illegitimacy rate amongst whites was 3 percent. Murray connects American behavior with these norms and values. He uses the 1963 Current Population Survey to make the point that "marriage was nearly universal and divorce rare across all races" and that "more than 80 percent of married women with children didn't work outside the home in 1963" (4). Murray uses this survey to make the point that rich and poor were connected in their view that "it was not respectable to be adult, male and idle. 98 percent of male respondents in these interviews said they were working or looking for work" (5).

Looking back from our current vantage point, we can see indications of the profound cultural changes that were to come and loosen many of these connections. The "discovery" of poverty, the civil rights movement, and the start of the feminist, consumer, and environmental movements all had their beginnings in the early sixties. Murray's point is that Americans in 1963 did not have the benefit of such hindsight (8).

Figure 5.3: Pattern of Connections: Picture of American Culture 1960s

NEW SOCIAL CLASSES AND *COMING APART*

Murray established the connections amongst Americans living in 1963 in order to argue that these connections were progressively loosened between 1960 and 2010. To make this case, he constructs two new social classes and tries to show that the separation between these classes is a social problem that needs to be addressed. In Durkheim's terms, it is indicative of anomie. *Coming Apart* is about the state of white America. Murray says he focuses his attention on white America for two reasons. First, he argues that during the last fifty years, white America has been used as a reference point from which to measure racial and ethnic differences in America. He thinks it may have "distracted our attention from the way the reference point itself is changing" (Murray 2012, 12). Second, he wants to emphasize that the social problem he addresses is about class, not race or ethnicity. "Don't kid yourself that we are looking at stresses that can be remedied by attacking the legacy of racism or by restricting immigration" (13).

The New Upper Class

Class is an intellectual construct. It is not something you can point to. Analysts construct class out of a combination of theoretical concepts, data, and argument. They use their particular way of combining these elements to connect people as belonging to the same social grouping. Sometimes the people so connected conceive of themselves as belonging to that grouping. Sometimes they don't.

Murray constructs his new upper class to connect a section of the US population by cognitive ability, educational background, occupation, geographical location, and lifestyle. He argues that the same connections that unite this section of the population separate them from the rest of the country.

Cognitive Ability

Murray employs his long-term curiosity about the social effects of innate intellectual differences to help him construct his new upper class. He establishes a baseline definition for a new category of workers that makes up an increasingly large section of the new upper- and upper-middle class. Different analysts have used different terms for this new category of workers—symbolic analyst, cognitive elite, the educated class, the creative class, mind workers. "The new class of symbolic analysts consisted of managers, engineers, attorneys, scientists, professors, executives, journalists, consultants, and other 'mind workers' whose work consists of processing information ... the new economy was ideally suited to their talents and rewarded them accordingly" (Murray 2012, 16).

Murray argues that changes in the economy over the last half century have vastly increased the market value of cognitive ability. He gives three reasons for this. First, the higher-tech the economy, the more openings there are for people with exceptional cognitive ability. Second, the more complex business decisions become, the greater the need for people with exceptional cognitive ability to make them. Third, the bigger the stakes, the greater the value of a marginal increase of skills becomes (47–48). As a result, "given the same interpersonal skills, energy, and common sense the manager with higher cognitive ability has an edge in increasing profitability by 10 percent instead of five percent—and that, combined with the larger stakes, also made brains worth more in the marketplace" (49).

HIGH INCOMES, NEW LIFESTYLES, AND INCREASED SEPARATION

Wealth and its inequitable distribution over the last thirty years provided the economic basis for Murray's new upper class, but wealth was only its enabler. "Just about all the benefits of economic growth went to people in the upper half of the income distribution … the increase was most dramatic at the very top of the distribution" (Murray 2012, 50). People in managerial occupations made a lot more money in 2010 than they did in 1960 and "their growing wealth enabled the most successful of them … to isolate themselves from the rest of America in ways that they formerly could not afford to do" (49).

Murray employs data to suggest that people who rank in the top 5 percent of income in the United States share "tastes, preferences, and culture" not shared by the rest of the population. He argues that, during the last half century, this cognitive elite has come to meet his two criteria for constituting a subculture. First, they are sufficient in number and share a distinctive set of tastes and preferences. Second, they are able to get together and form a critical mass large enough to shape a local scene (25). He tries to show that this group didn't meet these criteria in 1960. There weren't enough of these kinds of people then, they weren't concentrated enough geographically, and those holding management and professional positions didn't earn enough money and didn't have enough lifestyle choices to distinguish themselves from the rest of the population in the early 1960s. By 2010, he tries to show, they did. That is what he means by the new upper class (22).

Figure 5.4: American Upper Class

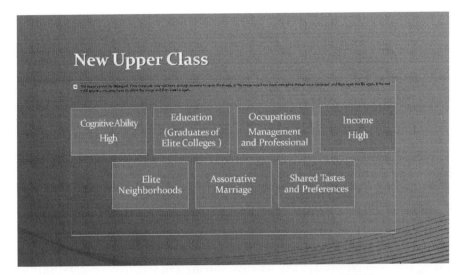

Figure 5.5: Pattern of Connections: American Upper Class 2010

It isn't always possible to find precisely the kind of data one needs to make the point one wants to make. Though he clearly prefers quantitative data, much of the data Murray employs to connect income, occupation, and educational attainment with shared tastes and preferences is qualitative. He insists that "much of the specialized quantitative information about the new elite's tastes and preferences exists. ... Everybody who sells advertising has detailed data on the demographics of consumer preferences ... but such data is proprietary" (35). The quantitative data he does use was provided by the worldwide advertising agency DDB. The DDB lifestyle data was first used by Robert Putnam (2000) for his book *Bowling Alone*. While the highest income level for this data is considerably lower ($100,000) than the minimum income for Murray's new upper class ($199,000) it gives a quantitative measure of the relationship between incomes, education, and consumer tastes and preferences (Murray, 2012, 35).

Murray cites this data, indicating that members of the new upper class prefer foreign to American cars; are thinner and more health conscious than the rest of the American population; prefer wine and boutique beer when they drink; rarely smoke; listen to different radio programs; watch far less television; and take different kinds of vacations in different places than does the population at large. They also marry at an older age and have fewer children (Murray 2012, 34–38).

Murray tries to show that the child-rearing practices of the new upper- and upper-middle class are different from those of the rest of the population. "Open affection, verbal interaction with infants and toddlers and consistent discipline ... on these and other good parenting practices social scientists find that, as groups, parents in the upper-middle class come out well ahead of parents in the middle and working classes" (39). More culturally significant still, in Murray's view, "a much larger proportion of working class than upper-middle class children are raised in broken or never formed homes" (40).

To supplement his quantitative data, Murray selects and describes television programs that depict this new upper-class subculture—*Thirtysomething, Mad About You, Ally McBeal, Frasier, The West Wing*. (There are plenty of more up-to-date shows that could provide the same illustration.) The characters in these shows display the characteristics of this new subculture. They have been educated at elite schools; they discuss intellectually esoteric subjects; their sex lives are emotionally complicated; the male characters are on the way up on the basis of flair and creativity; the female characters are conflicted about motherhood yet obsessed about being state-of-the-art moms (24).

Murray devises three kinds of what he calls "sorting mechanisms" to connect people together into the new upper class, and to separate the members of this class from the rest of the population: the college sorting machine, homogamy or assortative marriage, and the residential sorting machine.

The College Sorting Machine

Murray constructs the college sorting mechanism out of data he previously employed in *The Bell Curve* (Herrnstein and Murray 1994), data from Roger Geiger's (2002) *The Future of the City of Intellect* and Joseph Soares' (2007) *The Power of Privilege*. He uses this data to show that, until the 1960s, the student body in elite colleges and universities were connected by the socioeconomic status of their families, rather than by their cognitive ability. He uses average Scholastic Aptitude Test (SAT) scores of Harvard freshmen to demonstrate that by 1960 this had begun to change. The average SAT score of incoming Harvard freshmen went up almost 100 points between 1952 and 1960. Murray provides a quote from Harvard's dean of admissions in 1960, William G. Bender, who called the change "the greatest change in Harvard admissions ... in our recorded history" (Murray 2012, 55).

The clustering of students with high SAT scores in elite universities continued and accelerated during the next half century. Murray produces a chart to depict this clustering. It shows that 105 colleges and universities took 74 percent of students with SAT scores in the top 5 percent of all students who took the SATs. He produces a second chart indicating that a third-tier public university "is filled with students not much brighter than the average young person as a whole" (57).

Murray wants to show two things: first, that these exceptionally intellectually able students come predominantly from his new upper- and upper-middle class; and second, that "the children of the well-educated and affluent get most of the top scores because they constitute most of the smartest kids. They are smart in large part because their parents are smart" (61).

ASSORTATIVE MARRIAGE

Murray constructs a table based on data he takes from the National Longitudinal Study of Youth. His table presents a picture that connects the mean IQ of cohorts reaching adulthood in 1979 and 1997 with the educational attainment level of those cohorts. His table shows a correlation between IQ and level of educational attainment in both cohorts. Murray's conclusion is that the higher the IQ, the higher the level of educational attainment. Next, he wants to demonstrate "what happens when exceptionally able students all hang out together" (57). His answer is that they tend to marry one another. This is Murray's second sorting mechanism, homogamy or assortative marriage (61).

From this he concludes two things: first, if the mean IQ rises with the level of educational attainment, then the growth of two-degree couples will produce greater cognitive homogamy at the top; second, when people with high SAT scores attending elite schools marry other people with high SAT scores from elite schools, they will have children with IQs that will tend toward the mean of their parents (66). Thus, cognitive ability is transferred to the next generation.

Murray's (2012) conclusion? "Highly disproportionate numbers of exceptionally able children in the next generation will come from parents in the upper and upper-middle class" (68).

THE RESIDENTIAL SORTING MACHINE

Next, Murray wants to show that his new upper and upper-middle class are connected to each other by what he calls the "residential sorting machine" through which "they have separated themselves from just about everybody who isn't as rich and well educated as they are" (Murray 2012, 70).

He presents this phenomenon by creating a score combining education and income for every postal zip code in the United States. He uses this score to identify what he calls "SuperZips," zip codes in which the residents score in the 95th percentile of all zip codes. College degrees were held by 63 percent of the people living in the SuperZips, and their median income was $141,400. These percentages were both too low for everyone in these locations to qualify for Murray's purposes. There were almost four times as many people living in them than were in his upper class. His point is that the people in the upper class were living together along with others only slightly less educated and well off than they were.

The major social problem caused by the new upper class, as he has constructed it, is its virtual isolation from the rest of American society. In Murray's terms, the new upper class lives in a bubble. This is particularly troubling, in his view, because members of this class hold key positions in the country's major institutions. As a result, in Murray's view, the people who run America's most important institutions are pretty much completely isolated from the rest of the country.

Even more troubling, in Murray's view, is the growth over the past half century of a new lower class that is increasingly lacking the founding virtues (values and norms) that made the United States exceptional. We will look at how Murray constructed his new lower class, and why he thinks the growth of these two new classes is tearing the United States apart, in the next chapter.

STUDY QUESTIONS

1. What are Murray's curiosities, concerns, and passions?
2. What is Charles Murray's topic in *Coming Apart*?
3. How does Murray use these curiosities, concerns, and passions, and his sociological imagination, to transform his topic into a social problem?
4. Describe the social problem Murray addresses in *Coming Apart*.
5. How does Murray use the concepts of history, class, and culture to address his problem?
6. What kinds of data does Murray use to construct his picture of the shared culture that he says existed in the United States in the early 1960s?
7. How does Murray construct his new upper class?
8. What kinds of data does Murray use to construct his picture of the new American upper class?
9. What does Murray mean by sorting mechanisms, and how does he use them?

ASSIGNMENTS

1. By now you should be able to do the following with the study you are analyzing:
   a. Identify the curiosities, concerns, and passions of the study's author.
   b. Identify the topic of the study.

c. Describe how the author(s) of your study use their sociological imagination and their curiosities, concerns, and passions to address a social or intellectual problem.

SUGGESTED FURTHER READINGS

Murray, Charles. 2012. *Coming Apart*, 46–100 (The Foundations of the New Upper Class and a New Kind of Segregation). New York: Crown Publishing.

Brooks, David. 2000. *BoBos in Paradise*. New York: Simon and Schuster.

Reeves, Richard. 2015. "The Dangerous Separation of the American Upper Class." *Brookings Social Mobility Papers*, September 3. https://www.brookings.edu/series/social-mobility-papers/

Wilcox, W. Bradford, Robert I. Lerman, and Joseph Price. 2015. "Mobility and Money in the U.S. States: The Marriage Effect." *Brookings Social Mobility Papers*, December 7.

IMAGE CREDITS

CHAPTER 6

CHARLES MURRAY'S *COMING APART: THE STATE OF WHITE AMERICA, 1960–2010*

THE LOOSENING OF CULTURAL CONNECTIONS, PART II: THE MAKING OF THE NEW LOWER CLASS

Murray pictures the population of the United States in the 1960s as possessing a widely shared value and norm system based on four virtues—a belief in the nuclear family, industry, honesty, and religiosity. He argues that, regardless of income level or social status, most Americans living at this time not only believed in the value and norm system based on these virtues, but largely practiced them as well. In Durkheim's terms, America was in a normal or healthy state.

He wants to contrast the picture of how the United States looked and worked in 1960 with a picture of the United States in 2010. Americans in 2010, he tries to show, were no longer connected by a shared culture, but were instead increasingly divided into two new classes and class-based subcultures, each increasingly distant and unaware of the other. In Durkheim's terms, America was in a pathological or anomic state.

THE NEW LOWER CLASS

Murray constructs his new lower class out of people in the bottom 30 percent of income. Out of this bottom 30 percent, he selects all prime-age Americans (30–49) who fit at least one of the following criteria:

- Males who don't earn enough money in a year to keep two adults above the poverty line
- Females who are unmarried with children
- Prime-age adults who belong to no organizations whatsoever (Murray 2012, 229)

Figure 6.1: The New Lower Class

By creating this new lower class, Murray hopes to identify that section of the population which he sees as "problematic" for America's civic culture (226). He

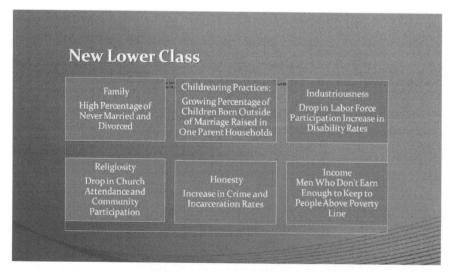

Figure 6.2: Pattern of Connections: The New Lower Class

wants to show that this section of the population lacks the founding virtues: belief in the nuclear family, industriousness, honesty, and religiosity.

MARRIAGE, FAMILY, AND CHILD-REARING PRACTICES IN THE NEW LOWER CLASS

Murray says that marriage is the fault line separating his two new classes. He uses the Current Population Survey to show that marriage rates in America took a nose-dive between 1970 and 1990. In 1970, 13 percent of white Americans between the ages of 30 and 49 were not living with their spouses; by 1990 that figure had jumped to 27 percent (Murray 2012, 154).

Murray uses data taken from the National Institute of Child Health and Human Development and Susan Brown's (2004, 2006) family studies to illustrate the negative effects of what he sees as the breakdown in the new lower class. "Both tell the same story: having two unmarried biological parents is associated with worse outcomes for children than having two married biological parents; and the outcomes were rarely better for children living with a single parent or in a 'cohabiting step-parent family'" (Murray, 2012, 165). Murray believes that families with children are the core around which communities must be organized, and that the structure of such families in his new lower class is collapsing (165).

THE DECLINE OF INDUSTRIOUSNESS IN THE NEW LOWER CLASS

Murray wants to show that the virtue of industriousness has been seriously eroded in his new lower class. Working hard, seeking to get ahead, and striving to be good at one's vocation define what Murray means by industriousness, and he thinks it is a founding American virtue. He also believes that it is a key to living a fulfilling life. Murray employs a combination of evidence and argument to show that this virtue eroded in the new lower class between 1960 and 2010. He uses the changes in answers to selected General Social Survey questions between 1973 and 2006; the rise in disability claims between 1960 and 2010; and the decline in labor force participation between 1960 and 2008 as signs of declining industriousness. He cites a change in what white people said they viewed as the most important factors in a job between 1973 and 2008. Between 1973 and 2008, the percentage of respondents who believed "a feeling of accomplishment" was the most important aspect of a job dropped from 58 percent to 43 percent; the percentage of respondents who

*Pg 63
*read of
rest of paragraph

answered that short working hours and no danger of being fired were the most important aspects of a job rose from 10 to 21 percent during the same time period (Murray 2012, 169). While admitting that "we can't be sure," Murray concludes that "it looks as if during the last half of the 1990s and the first half of the 2000s whites ... became less interested in meaningful work and more interested in secure jobs with short working hours" (170).

Next, Murray argues that because of improvements in medical care, the percentage of "workers who actually are physically or emotionally unable to work for reasons beyond their control has necessarily gone down since 1960" (170). Yet the percentage of workers qualifying for federal disability benefits for these reasons has risen from 0.7 percent to 5.3 percent. Murray concludes that the "real" reason for the rise in disability claims is loss of industriousness (171).

*Read Para.

Murray cites data on the decline in participation in the workforce between 1960 and 2008 as an indicator of the erosion of industriousness in white men between the ages of 30 and 49. The percentage of white men out of the workforce increased over three times during this period (173). This reduction of workforce participation affected men with low education much more than men with high education (173). "Throughout the 1960s American white males of all educational levels inhabited the same world. Starting in the 1970s they increasingly did not. By 2008 12 percent of American males with only a high school education had dropped out of the workforce while only three percent of those with a college degree had" (174).

Murray grants that the labor market for prime-age, lower-class white males changed during this period. Their pay level dropped dramatically. He argues, however, that if lower-class white men were industrious, this drop in pay shouldn't have resulted in the reduction of hours worked or in the increase in the percentage of those who dropped out of the workforce. "On the contrary: Insofar as men need work to survive ... falling hourly income does not discourage work" (178).

DECLINE OF INDUSTRIOUSNESS AND THE COLLAPSE OF THE FAMILY IN THE NEW LOWER CLASS

Murray posits a connection between the drop in industriousness and the drop in the number of married men. "Single prime age men are more than three times as likely to be out of the labor force." This was as true in 1960 as in 2010. "Put plainly, single prime aged men are much less industrious than married men" (183). From this, Murray concludes that there is clearly a connection between the decline in labor force participation and marriage. He, however, grants the possibility that this might

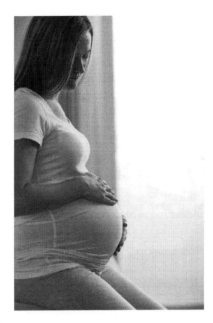

Figure 6.3: Single Mother

in part be because men who sees themselves as poor providers may be less likely to marry (183).

CRIME RATES AND THE DECLINE OF HONESTY IN THE NEW LOWER CLASS

Murray equates honesty, or rather dishonesty, with crime rates. Most of the national growth in white crime and imprisonment was concentrated in the new lower class (190). American crime during this period scarcely affected the new upper class at all (194).

While the crime rate in lower-class communities has dropped since the mid-1990s, the level of arrests, especially for violent crime, remains far above that of previous decades. Murray suggests that "the reduction in crime has occurred at the same time that large numbers of [lower-class] males have been taken off the streets and put into prison and to some degree because they are no longer around to victimize their neighbors" (194). He concludes that "lots more prisoners, lots more probationers, lots more parolees, and somewhat diminished arrests probably means that, taken together, the rise in criminality in [lower-class communities] continues" (194).

DECLINE IN RELIGIOSITY

Murray wants to say that religiosity has declined amongst his new lower class while remaining high amongst his new upper class. He has a difficult time doing so. Religiosity was a central aspect of the civic culture which united Americans in the 1960s. A number of studies since then have indicated its importance in maintaining cultural connections. Citing the work of Robert Putnam (2000), Murray argues that religiosity is a major contributor to social capital. Nearly half of all associational membership is church related, and much of personal philanthropy and volunteering occurs within a religious context (Murray, 2012, 200). Moreover, not only do church activities act as a kind of training for important civic skills, but "religious faith is empirically associated with good things such as better physical health, mental health, and longevity" (201).

The widely held view that religiosity is declining amongst the upper class, while maintaining its hold on lower-class Americans, doesn't fit well with Murray's views on what is tearing America apart. However, many of the data sources he uses to construct his picture of America in the 1960s support a good part of this widely held view. To counteract this view, Murray uses the terms "secular" and "religious" differently (204). The percentage of "hard-core" secular men between ages 30 and 49 (those who, when asked about their religious preferences, said "none") has sky-rocketed from one percent in 1963 to 21 percent in 2010. Murray grants that this trend "represents a rare instance of convergence" between his upper class and his lower class (203). He argues, however, that if we include those who say they are religious but don't go to church regularly amongst the secular, then the drift away from religion is far greater within the lower class than the upper class (204). Putting all this together, Murray maintains that "the critical mass" for generating the social capital (25–30%) continues to exist in upper-class communities but no longer does in lower-class communities (12%).

WHAT WOULD HAVE TO CHANGE TO SOLVE THE PROBLEM OF AMERICA'S FRACTURING CIVIC CULTURE?

Murray summarizes his view of the forces responsible for the fracturing of American civic culture in the following terms:

> On one side of the spectrum, a significant and growing portion of the American population is losing the virtues required to be functioning members of a free society. On the other side of the spectrum, the people

who run the country are doing just fine. Their framework for pursuing happiness is relatively unaffected by the forces that are enfeebling family, community, vocation and faith elsewhere in the society. In fact, they have become so isolated that they are often oblivious to the nature of the problems that exist elsewhere. ... The new upper class is showing signs of becoming an elite which is hollow to the core. (Murray 2012, 285)

Murray complains that instead of preaching the virtues that they, on the whole, practice, the new upper class maintains a position of "nonjudgmentalism" and "ecumenical niceness" (289). Moreover, the financial compensation of the new upper class has become, in cultural terms, "unseemly." "Unseemliness is a symptom of the collapse of codes of behavior that depend not on laws and regulations, but on shared understandings regarding the fitness of things, and upon an allegiance to behavior in accordance with those shared understandings. Unseemliness is another symptom of hollowness at the core" (294).

For America's civic culture to come together again, Murray says the people in his new upper class must regain the self-confidence to preach and advocate the founding virtues they still largely practice, but which they are careful not to espouse. Though he doesn't use the term, Murray urges his new upper class to become a ruling class that makes its values and norms the values and norms of American society as a whole.

Should a significant portion of the new upper class take on this responsibility in the future, Murray thinks they will have ideological weapons at their disposal which they do not now have. He predicts that advances in sociobiology and cognitive science will produce a "title wave of scientific understanding of human behavior" that will provide scientific support for the American project and discredit its alternative, the welfare state. Murray also predicts that the world will witness the financial and eventually economic and cultural collapse of the European welfare state (296).

Armed with advances in sociobiology and cognitive science, and the collapse of the leading alternative to the American project (the European welfare state), it is possible, Murray argues, that elements of the new upper class may regain their courage and lead a new religiously based social movement that will put American civic culture back together (303–305).

THE SOCIAL THEORIZING IN MURRAY'S *COMING APART*: EVALUATION

Murray makes no attempt to take a neutral stance on the problem he addresses. Instead of trying to put his curiosities, concerns, and passions aside, he uses them to guide and inform his work. This doesn't necessarily mean he isn't objective. His objectivity should be judged by the forthrightness of the perspective he takes toward his study, the honesty with which he attempts to address alternative perspectives of his problem, and the fairness with which he tries to do so.

When we analyze the theorizing presented to us by authors who take perspectives different from our own, we shouldn't feel obliged either to ignore the author's perspective or to pretend we don't have an alternate one. A good rule of thumb in trying to perform objective analysis in social theorizing is to try to make the best possible case for theorizing from perspectives different from your own, and to be as critical as possible in your analysis of theorizing done from perspectives you share. Because I am far more sympathetic to social democracy than I am to Murray's right, libertarian perspective, I have tried to make the best possible case for the theorizing Murray does in *Coming Apart*.

In constructing his picture of how America looks and works, Murray is careful to include studies of authors with perspectives different from his own. Though a staunch opponent of social democracy, he employs Robert Reich's (Secretary of Labor in the Clinton administration) concepts of the symbolic analyst and the succession of the successful. He has high praise for Theda Skocpol's (left-leaning social analyst) *Diminished Democracy* (2003). Both Reich and Skocpol approach the topics addressed in *Coming Apart* from perspectives very different from Murray's. As part of his critique of the European model of social democracy, Murray devotes a page listing "thoughtful and useful analyses of the European model which are supportive of it" (280).

Murray does not ignore inconvenient facts. He grants that all whites, not just those in the new lower class, have begun to be more interested in shorter working hours and job security than meaningful work (170). When he discusses honesty, he admits that he has been unable to determine whether the well-publicized cases of corporate corruption are indicative of a decline in honesty in the new upper class (196).

How Changing the Zero Point Might Alter the Picture

Murray begins his account of American social life by establishing a historical zero point, the point at which the phenomena he studies did not yet exist. Murray uses the early 1960s as his zero point. At this point, Murray argues, American civic culture was intact and looked much as it had always looked since the country's founding. He makes a persuasive case for the intactness of America's civic culture in the early 1960s—but would that case have been as compelling had he chosen a different zero point? The early 1960s marks the high point of a historical era that is often called the Great Compression. Economic inequality decreased considerably between the 1940s and the 1960s, and then expanded greatly beginning in the 1970s, until, in 1985, it had risen back to where it had been at the beginning of the twentieth century (Goldin and Margo 1991). As a result, it may be that the strength of American civic culture was a characteristic of one period in American history rather than all of it.

Objective Measures of Subjective States

Murray's picture of American civic culture includes shared ideas, values, norms, attitudes, and sentiments, as well as material artifacts like cars and televisions. He identifies the ideal elements in the culture (like the virtues of industriousness, honesty, belief in the nuclear family, and religiosity) through objective quantitative measures: hours worked, percentage of population collecting disability benefits, crime and incarceration rates. He measures religiosity through answers to survey questions that ask respondents about their religious preferences and how long it has been since they went to church.

There is nothing wrong with employing such measures, as long as we realize that they are **objective indicators of subjective states**. Does the number of hours per week a person works completely capture the subjective state of industriousness? That of course depends on what we mean by industriousness. Is religiosity successfully captured by statements of adherence to or attendance at a particular church? It is certainly possible to define the one in terms of the other (which is what Murray does), but it is also possible to use the term religious very differently, as a synonym for spiritual, for instance. One might well be spiritual without claiming adherence to, or attending, any particular church. I think Murray is at his least convincing when he tries to argue that his new upper class remains "religious enough" in 2010, while his new lower class does not. The evidence seems to me to indicate that religiosity has dropped significantly amongst Americans as a whole, not just among his new lower class. While changing the definition changes the picture, it can also distort it. Given the evidence, it would seem that if members of the new upper class are to lead a religious awakening, they will have a steep climb.

Do Crime and Incarceration Rates Measure Honesty or Something Else?

I also find the use of crime and incarceration rates as measures of honesty (actually, dishonesty) troubling and unconvincing. As we will see in the next chapter, crime rates go up or down in response to a number of factors other than a rise or fall in the honesty of a population. When the number of police is increased, arrests go up. When they are concentrated in particular neighborhoods, the arrest rates in those neighborhoods go up. When prosecutors and judges "get tough on crime," the number of people imprisoned and the length of their sentences goes up. It seems to me quite possible for honest people to be arrested, convicted of a crime, and sent to prison. It also seems to me quite possible for dishonest people to not be arrested, convicted of a crime, or sent to prison. So, I'm not convinced that an increase in arrest, conviction, and incarceration rates in poor neighborhoods indicates a decline in honesty.

I am also not convinced that low crime rates in wealthy neighborhoods are a reliable indicator of the honesty of those who live there. When police, prosecutors, and judges in the 1970s got tough on crime, they didn't do so in rich neighborhoods; they did so in poor ones. Murray admits that he is unable determine whether or not the well-publicized cases of massive corporate crime indicate a rise in dishonesty in the new upper class. However, he is willing to let "sharp" business practices (Murray 2012, 194–95), a certain level of sexual harassment (8), and the propensity to use violence to settle disputes (133) slide on the honesty scale, as long as they don't result in arrest and conviction for a crime.

IQs and SATs: I'm Rich Because I'm Smart

Murray uses IQ and SAT scores as indicators of cognitive abilities. We should keep in mind that there are plenty of people who question IQ as a measure of intelligence. Murray himself now thinks SATs should be abandoned.

Murray attributes the high salaries given to the "cognitive elite" to the increasing value of intellect in the marketplace. There are, however, other possible explanations.

The chief executives of major corporations have their compensation packages determined by corporate boards composed of people like themselves. Such boards have been known to award significant raises to executives with questionable performance records. The same can be said of the awarding of bonuses in the financial industry.

CHANGING PLACES: "IF I WERE POOR I'D WORK HARDER"

Murray has a good awareness of the audience he is addressing in *Coming Apart*. He recognizes that the readers of a book like his are likely to be members of the new upper and upper-middle class.

Murray asks his readers to put themselves in the place of a lower-class man only qualified for low-skill jobs. He concludes that the reader would work at whatever job was available for as many hours as possible. Putting oneself in the position of another relies on a capacity for empathy, a capacity on which people differ. Moreover, whatever conclusion the reader might reach through exercising this capacity would be impossible to verify. What you would have done had you been in the situation of another is impossible to say, because you weren't.

CLASS SEPARATION: HOW DEEP IS THE VALLEY?

What Murray succeeds in establishing in *Coming Apart* is that narrow elite, broader elite, and the upper-middle class (approximately 20 percent of the population) are connected to each other. They circulate and have a good understanding of each other. The same could be said of the working class and the new lower class. If America is coming apart, the crucial separation would appear to be between the new upper-middle class and the working class. Yet this is a subject Murray doesn't explore.

In fairness, Murray says that "discussing solutions is secondary to this book" (13). That said, it's hard to see how a religious awakening would solve the problem of the class-based and increasingly distant subcultures *Coming Apart* describes while the income gap enabling these subcultures persists. The American project Murray trumpets, and the civic culture that he sees as coming apart, were rooted in the shared national belief in widespread opportunity. At least implicitly, Murray's religious awakening would appear at best to suggest the possibility of a shared culture based on lower-class acceptance of their lot, rather than in a widespread belief in the opportunity for class mobility. Is that the American project?

STUDY QUESTIONS

1. How does Murray create his new lower class?
2. How does Murray suggest that the coming apart of America might be halted?
3. How would you evaluate the theorizing Murray does in *Coming Apart*?

ASSIGNMENT

1. Describe the major methodological approach you intend to take in your research project. What major concepts and kinds of data do you plan to use? If you plan on creating your own data, describe the major techniques you intend to employ to do so. If you intend to use existing data sources, identify them.

FURTHER SUGGESTED READINGS

Hochschild, Arlie. 2016. "I Spent 5 Years with Some of Trump's Biggest Fans. Here's What They Won't Tell You." *Mother Jones*, September/October.www. motherjones.com/politics/2016/08/trump-white-blue-collar-supporters

Murray, Charles. 2012. *Coming Apart: The State of White America, 1960–2010*, 144–209 (Marriage, Industriousness, Honesty and Religion). New York: Crown Publishing.

Putnam, Robert. 2015. *Our Kids*, 1–46 (Introduction). New York: Simon and Schuster.

Vance, J. D. 2016. *Hillbilly Elegy*, 47–60 (Chapter 4). New York: Harper Collins.

IMAGE CREDITS

CHAPTER 7

MICHELLE ALEXANDER'S *THE NEW JIM CROW: MASS INCARCERATION IN THE AGE OF COLORBLINDNESS*

THE CONSTRUCTION OF A RACIALIZED CASTE, PART I: SLAVERY AND JIM CROW SEGREGATION

Like Charles Murray, Michelle Alexander has her curiosities, concerns, and passions. The curiosity that sparked her study *The New Jim Crow* was a sign she noticed nailed to a telephone pole in Oakland, California. The sign announced a community meeting sponsored by a local radical group, and said, "The Drug War is the New Jim Crow" (Alexander 2012, 3). She initially dismissed the sign as an example of the hyperbolic tendencies of a lot of radical groups. Still, it made her curious. The more she thought about the sign, the more curious she became.

At the time she saw the sign, Michelle Alexander was a young civil rights lawyer concerned about attacks on affirmative action policies and what she then saw as the lingering effects of segregation on African Americans. "I understood the problems plaguing poor communities of color, including problems associated with crime and rising incarceration rates, to be a function of poverty and lack of access to quality education" (3). She was and is a passionate advocate for the civil, social, and economic rights of African Americans, and of an egalitarian society.

INTELLECTUAL AND SOCIAL PROBLEM ADDRESSED

As we will see below, Alexander's study addresses an intellectual as well as a social problem. The thinking, research, and interviewing that resulted in *The New Jim Crow* led her to conclude that she was wrong about the connection between African American crime, rising incarceration rates, and the legacy of segregation. She no longer thinks that crime and rising incarceration rates in poor African American communities are vestiges of the old Jim Crow. She now thinks they are crucial aspects of the new Jim Crow.

Concepts: Caste, Class, and Race

Charles Murray constructs two new classes to paint his picture of how the contemporary United States looks and works. Alexander constructs a new conception of caste and a new definition of mass incarceration to paint a very different picture. In texts like those we surveyed in Chapter 3, caste is presented as a system of social stratification sometimes found in traditional societies. Traditional India is usually given as the example of a social system once governed by a caste system. (The caste system is officially outlawed in contemporary India, though it still has important effects on social life.) India's caste system is probably thousands of years old and is connected with the Hindu religion. Introductory sociology texts make the point that caste systems like India's are closed systems in which one's status is given for life and is based on one's parents' position in the system. Caste systems are usually contrasted with class-based systems of stratification, which are presented as characteristic of modern developed societies. Class systems are conceived of as open systems in which one's position is determined by achieved characteristics, particularly income and wealth. Class systems are open in the sense that it is possible to change one's position in the system during one's lifetime.

Alexander constructs her own conception of caste and uses it to make sense of the position of African Americans throughout American history. Alexander's uses the concept of caste not to denote a system of stratification, but to characterize a form of social control. "I use the term racial caste … to denote a stigmatized racial group locked into an inferior position by law and custom" (Alexander 2012, 12).

Historical Narrative

Like Murray's, Alexander's study has a historical dimension. However, she conceptualizes the historical dimension of human social life differently than does Murray. Murray establishes a historical zero point—a point at which the phenomenon he studied, the coming apart of American civic culture, had not yet begun. Alexander uses her concept of caste to construct a narrative that she employs to present a picture of the recurring features characterizing the historical experience of African Americans in the United States. In effect, Alexander uses the historical narrative she constructs to answer a question: is there a way to think of slavery, Jim Crow segregation, and mass incarceration as different instances of the same caste system? To answer her question affirmatively, she "conceives of each as a caste system which takes different forms in different historical periods. … Jim Crow and slavery were caste systems. So is our current system of mass incarceration" (Alexander 2012, 12).

THE CONCEPT OF RACIAL CASTE

Race is the ascribed characteristic upon which Alexander builds her concept of caste. She argues that the status of African Americans is determined by the ascribed characteristic of race. She conceives of racialized caste as a closed system that circumscribes the position and status of African Americans in the American social hierarchy. In the caste Alexander has constructed, race is inherited from one's parents and passed on to one's children. African Americans are assigned throughout their lives to the lowest position in American society, one outside and beneath the class system. Alexander pictures African Americans as the United States' untouchables. Like India's untouchables, their caste position is enforced and maintained by law and custom.

MASS INCARCERATION AS A FORM OF RACIALIZED CASTE

Alexander pictures African American slavery and Jim Crow segregation as different forms of racialized caste, one form historically following the other. Her central task in *The New Jim Crow* is to show that mass incarceration is another form of racialized caste, one that historically followed that of Jim Crow segregation. She understands that, on the face of it, this doesn't seem to make sense. At first it didn't make sense to her. "Only after years of working on criminal justice reform did my own focus finally shift, and then the rigid caste system slowly came into view" (Alexander 2012, 12). It was not the social world that changed; it was the way Alexander came to view it that led her to "see" this caste system. It is in this sense that the problem Alexander addresses in *The New Jim Crow* is intellectual as well as social.

This new way of viewing the social world involved conceiving of what she meant by "mass incarceration" differently. "The term mass incarceration refers not only to the criminal justice system but also to the larger web of laws, rules, policies and customs that control those labeled criminals both in and out of prison. Once released, former prisoners enter into a hidden underworld of legalized discrimination and permanent social exclusion. They are members of America's new undercaste" (13). To make her point, she must address the following kinds of objections: (1) surely the status of criminal is achieved, not ascribed; and (2) criminals earn their status the same way middle-class professionals earn theirs. These objections can be refuted if you alter the way you look at the social world in the way Alexander has. She presents her readers with a picture of an American social world in which gaining the status of criminal is a matter of race, not behavior. Central to Alexander's picture is a new conception of the American criminal justice system and how it works.

> The current system of control permanently locks a huge percentage of the African-American community out of the mainstream society and economy. The system operates through our criminal justice institutions, but it functions more like a caste system than a system of control. ... Although this new system of racialized social control purports to be colorblind; it creates and maintains racial hierarchy much as earlier systems of social control did. Like Jim Crow (and slavery) mass incarceration operates as a tightly networked system of laws, policies, customs and institutions that operate collectively to ensure the subordinate status of a group defined largely by race. (13)

SLAVERY, RACE, AND SOCIAL CONFLICT

Alexander uses caste to compare the way mass incarceration came into existence with the way slavery and Jim Crow segregation came into being. To do so, she adopts what sociology texts call a **conflict perspective**. By contrast, Charles Murray takes what those same texts call a **consensus perspective**. Like Durkheim, Murray looks for what ties people together—a civic culture—and then examines how those ties sometimes fall apart. Like Marx and Weber, Alexander looks at the human social world as an arena of conflict within which social groups struggle for power, wealth, and prestige. When she looks at human social life, she tries to identify the groups that are struggling; what they are struggling over; who wins and who loses; and the social consequences of their victories and defeats. Tenuous periods of consensus are reached when one group or coalition of groups is able to successfully work its will over and above the resistance of other groups.

THE LAWYER'S BRIEF: DATA

Alexander is a lawyer by profession. Her book takes the form of a brief in which she gathers all the evidence she can to make her case. She doesn't bother looking for inconvenient facts that might weaken her case. Accustomed to working within the adversarial American system of justice, she seems to leave that task to her adversaries. Alexander is not a social scientist. With the exception of her citation of court cases, the data she employs consists mainly of secondary sources: books and newspaper and journal articles written by others.

SLAVERY AS A FORM OF RACIALIZED CASTE

Figure 7.1: Slavery

Alexander employs the conflict perspective and the concept of racialized caste along with data taken from the works of historians like Edmond Morgan (1975), Charles Vann Woodward (1955), and Gerald Fresia (1998) to construct a picture of slavery as a form of racialized social control emerging out of a conflict between indigenous peoples, indentured servants, free immigrants, and Southern planters during the early colonial period of American history. Southern landowners wanted to build plantations on which to grow commercial crops like tobacco, rice, and, particularly, cotton. They found indigenous peoples and indentured servants unsuitable as a labor force. They turned instead to the importation of African slaves to work their lands.

CONCEPT: THE RACIAL BRIBE

At the time, Alexander argues, indentured servants were not distinguished by race (Alexander 2012, 23). Southern planters employed a "racial bribe" to divide indentured servants by race and then turn them against indigenous peoples. They bribed white indentured servants by encouraging and supporting their efforts to confiscate the lands owned by indigenous peoples. Slavery and taking land from indigenous peoples was justified by the invention of racism and white supremacy. If indigenous peoples were viewed as "wild savages" and "redskins" inferior to civilized white Europeans and their descendants, the confiscation of their lands could be justified. If Africans were seen as an inferior race, their enslavement could be justified. Alexander argues that rich Southern planters won over poor whites by offering them land confiscated from an inferior race of "redskins" and a status superior to that of African slaves (23–25).

In Alexander's historical narrative, the establishment of the United States is pictured as the result of a compromise between conflicting elites in the former Southern and Northern colonies. The US Constitution granted the central government (the federal government) increased power, which elites in the North wanted and those in the South had resisted in exchange for the de facto recognition of a racial caste of African slaves in many of the Southern states.

ABOLITION, RECONSTRUCTION, CLASS, AND RACIAL CONFLICT

Alexander has surprisingly little to say about the American Civil War and the contribution of the interracial abolitionist and radical republican social movements to the abolition of slavery. She has more to say about the brief period of Reconstruction that followed the end of the Civil War and the abolition of slavery. In Alexander's historical narrative, the Reconstruction period is seen as a time when racialized caste might have been eliminated but ultimately wasn't.

> The Reconstruction Era ... did appear at least for a time to have the potential to seriously undermine, if not completely eradicate, the racial caste system in the South. With the protection of federal troops, African Americans began to vote in large numbers and seize control, in some areas, of the local political apparatus. Literacy rates climbed, and educated blacks began to populate legislatures, open schools, and initiate successful businesses. In 1867 at the dawn of the Reconstruction Era, no black man

Figure 7.2: Black Reconstruction

held political office in the South, yet fifteen years later, at least 15 percent of all Southern elected officials were black. (Alexander 2012, 29)

POPULISM, RACE, AND CLASS CONFLICT

In Alexander's narrative, the early years of the Populist movement are seen as containing the possibility of an interracial movement of poor people capable of challenging white elites in the South. Alexander selects parts of a speech given by Tom Watson, a Populist leader, to show this early Populist possibility. In it, Watson calls for a union of black and white farmers: "You are apart that you might be separately fleeced of your earnings. You are made to hate each other because upon the hatred is rested the keystone of the arch of financial despotism that enslaves you both. You are deceived and blinded that you may not see how this race antagonism perpetuates a monetary system which beggars you both" (33).

Alexander pictures Populism, in its beginnings, as a budding multiracial social movement. Alexander employs a quote from C. Vann Woodward (1955), the author of *The Strange Career of Jim Crow*, to bolster this view of Populism: "It is altogether probable that during the brief Populist upheaval of the [eighteen] nineties Negroes and native whites achieved a greater comity of mind and harmony of political purpose than ever before or since in the South" (33).

JIM CROW SEGREGATION, RACE, AND CLASS CONFLICT

Figure 7.3: Jim Crow

In Alexander's narrative, Jim Crow segregation is seen as the result of the defeat of the Populist coalition of poor blacks and whites by rich Southern white elites. "Just as the white elite had successfully driven a wedge between poor whites and blacks ... by creating the institution of black slavery, another racial caste system was emerging two centuries later, in part due to the efforts of white elites to decimate a multiracial alliance of poor people" (35).

At the beginning of the twentieth century all Southern states had laws that effectively denied blacks the right to vote and segregated them in virtually all aspects of life—schools, churches, housing, jobs, restaurants, hotels, even drinking fountains, morgues, and orphanages (35). In Alexander's narrative, the new form of racialized caste, Jim Crow segregation, had replaced slavery as the form of racial caste in the South.

THE CIVIL RIGHTS MOVEMENT, CLASS CONFLICT, AND THE DEFEAT OF JIM CROW

Figure 7.4: Civil Rights Movement

The next chapter in Alexander's narrative begins during and directly after World War II. In her picture, this period is defined by the formation of a new interracial coalition of forces that challenge Jim Crow segregation in the South. The mass migration of African Americans out of the rural South; the experience of other African Americans in the Armed Forces; steps toward the integration of the United States Armed Forces; and legal challenges by the National Association for the Advancement of Colored People (NAACP) to segregation all contributed to the formation of this coalition.

Alexander pictures the 1954 Supreme Court decision *Brown v. Board of Education* as signaling to white segregationists a real threat to Jim Crow segregation in the South. "Brown threatened not only to end segregation in public schools, but also, by implication, the entire system of legalized segregation in the South" (Alexander 2012, 36). In response, Southern segregationists mounted a sustained and multi-fronted defense of "their way of life." A Southern Manifesto vowing to maintain segregation by all legal means was signed by 101 out of the 128 members of Congress representing the original Confederate states. White citizens, councils composed primarily of upper- and middle-class white businessmen and clergy were formed in most Southern cities. A revitalized Ku Klux Klan engaged in a campaign of illegal violence against those who supported integration in the South. Southern legislators passed new Jim Crow laws (37).

The segregationist forces were opposed by a growing coalition of white and black activists, who launched a campaign of boycotts, marches, sit-ins, and black voter registration drives challenging Jim Crow laws throughout the South. A bitter, protracted conflict between these two forces ensued, involving nonviolent civil disobedience on the part of the civil rights movement, and arrests and mob violence on the part of their opponents. Much of this struggle was covered in newspaper stories and television reports throughout the world. Alexander, as did Murray, identifies 1963 as a key turning point in American history. "The dramatic high point of the Civil Rights Movement occurred in 1963. The Southern struggle had grown from a modest group of black students demonstrating peacefully at one lunch counter to the largest mass movement for racial reform and civil rights in the twentieth century" (37). On June 12, 1963, President Kennedy announced that he would present a strong Civil Rights Bill before Congress. After Kennedy's assassination, President Johnson announced his commitment to the goal of "full assimilation of more than twenty million Negroes into American life" (38). Under his leadership the Civil Rights Act of 1964 and the Voting Rights Act of 1965 were passed, essentially ending Jim Crow segregation as a form of racial caste.

The Poor Peoples Movement That Wasn't

The same coalition of groups that defeated Jim Crow in the South next attempted to wage a nationwide struggle for the economic rights of poor people. President Johnson responded with the announcement of an "unconditional war on poverty" and led the struggle to pass the Economic Opportunity Act of 1964. "As the Civil Rights Movement began to evolve into a 'Poor Peoples Movement' it promised to address not only black poverty but white poverty as well—thus raising the specter of a poor and working class movement that cut across racial lines" (Alexander 2012, 39).

In the next chapter, we will examine how, in Alexander's view, white conservative elites used the rhetoric of law and order and the War on Drugs to create a new form of racialized caste to prevent this from happening.

Study Questions

1. What are Alexander's curiosities, concerns, and passions?
2. If race and crime are the topics of Alexander's study, what is the problem the book addresses? Why is it an intellectual as well as a social problem?

3. What are the major concepts Alexander employs in the construction of the first two parts of her historical narrative?

4. What does Michelle Alexander mean by racialized caste? How does she use this concept to organize her historical narrative?

5. Describe the social forces which, according to Alexander, were responsible for the creation of slavery and Jim Crow segregation as forms of racialized caste.

6. What is the difference between a conflict and a consensus perspective? Which one does Murray employ? Which one does Alexander employ? How does each employ their perspective?

ASSIGNMENT

1. Determine whether the author(s) of the study you are analyzing employ a conflict or a consensus perspective.

2. Describe the methodical approach to you intend to take in your project. Be sure to include whether you intend to employ a conflict or a consensus perspective (or combination of both) if you think it relevant.

SUGGESTED FURTHER READINGS

Alexander, Michelle. 2012. *The New Jim Crow: Mass Incarceration in the Age of Colorblindness*, rev. ed., 20–58 (The Rebirth of Caste). New York: The New Press.

Stamp, Kenneth. 1965. *The Era of Reconstruction: 1865–1877*, 155–217 (Radical Rule in the South and the Triumph of the Conservatives). New York: Random House.

Woodward, C. Vann. 1955. *The Strange Career of Jim Crow*, 31–111 (Forgotten Alternatives and Capitulation to Racism). New York: Oxford University Press.

IMAGE CREDITS

Fig. 7.1: Henry P. Moore, "Slavery." Copyright in the Public Domain.

CHAPTER 8

MICHELLE ALEXANDER'S *THE NEW JIM CROW: MASS INCARCERATION IN THE AGE OF COLORBLINDNESS*

CLASS, IDEOLOGICAL CONFLICT, LAW, AND ORDER, PART II: THE BIRTH OF THE NEW JIM CROW

According to Alexander, the prospect of white, black, and ethnic poor people demanding a more egalitarian society precipitated the conflict between twentieth-century liberals and the contemporary conservative movement. As they had in the past, in Alexander's view, white elites used racism to divide the poor. White elites coalescing around a resurgent conservative movement recognized that the efforts to construct a new form of racial caste would have to be conveyed in race neutral language. The language they selected was the language of "law and order." Instead of defending the old Jim Crow segregation, conservatives attacked the means the civil rights movement employed to oppose it. They argued that the civil disobedience engaged in by civil rights activists fostered an atmosphere of lawlessness. To do so, they connected civil disobedience, rioting in black neighborhoods in Northern cities, and the significant rise in street crime as different forms of the same thing.

The debate over how crime rates were calculated and what caused the increases in crime and disorder were part of the ideological conflict between conservatives and liberals. Alexander clearly sides with liberals in this conflict. She distinguishes between the "rioting" that occurred in Harlem and Rochester, New York, with the "rebellions" that occurred in many black urban communities after the assassination of Martin Luther King (Alexander 2012, 41). Alexander grants that there was significant rise in crime in Northern cities in the 1960s (street crime quadrupled and homicide rates doubled). She argues, however, that the increase in crime "can be explained by the rise of the baby boomer generation" and the rise in unemployment rates amongst black youth (41). She adds that "wide spread police brutality and abuse" in African American communities was "directly related" to the "uprisings" in black communities (42).

Alexander complains that these factors were not explored by the media at the time. Instead, she says, they sensationalized the rise in crime and attributed it to "the breakdown in lawfulness, morality, and social stability in the wake of the Civil

Rights Movement" (41). The conflict over how to respond to the rise in crime in black communities not only was part of the conflict between liberals and conservatives, it also caused a conflict amongst black activists (42).

LAW AND ORDER AND RACIAL CONTROL

According to Alexander's narrative, demands for "law and order" and to "get tough on crime" were really calls for the establishment of a new form of racialized caste. In defense of this argument, she says that the most ardent opponents of civil rights legislation and desegregation were the most active on the emerging crime issue (Alexander 2012, 42). She adds that ardent segregationists "led the legislative battle to curb rights of criminal defendants" (43).

From Alexander's angle of vision "a new race neutral language was developed for appealing to old racist sentiments, a language accompanied by a political movement that succeeded in putting blacks in their place. Proponents of racial hierarchy found they could install a new racial caste system without violating the law or new limits of acceptable political discourse, by demanding 'law and order' rather than 'segregation forever'" (40).

When placed within Alexander's narrative, the shift in public debate from segregation to crime left the battle lines "largely the same." "Positions taken on crime policies typically cohered along lines of racial ideology" (43). She cites a study indicating that legislators who opposed open housing, bussing, and the Civil Rights Act also voted for amendments to crime bills (43). Moreover, members of Congress who voted against civil rights measures proactively designed and backed crime measures as well (43).

Alexander points out that during the 1930s the Democratic Party formed a New Deal coalition consisting of ethnic groups in Northern cities (including blacks living in those cities) and Southern Democrats that dominated Congress for fifty years. In the 1980s, conservatives in the Republican Party used law-and-order rhetoric as part of a "Southern Strategy" designed to break apart this coalition and replace it with a new Republican conservative majority. This strategy was outlined by Kevin Phillips (1969) in *The Emerging Republican Majority*. While Phillips' suggested strategy was a good deal more complex and intricate than Alexander indicates, it certainly did include combining the traditional Republican base, whites in the South disenchanted with the Democratic Party's support of civil rights legislation, and a percentage of Catholic, blue collar voters in big cities (Alexander, 2012, 34).

The struggle between liberal Democrats and conservative Republicans was in part an ideological struggle based on two different pictures of the United States, each composed of a different pattern of connections. Liberal Democrats made connections between rising crime rates, poverty, and unemployment, particularly in urban black communities. Conservative Republicans connected rising crime to a culture of poverty and government social programs designed to assist the poor—again, particularly poor blacks in urban areas (45).

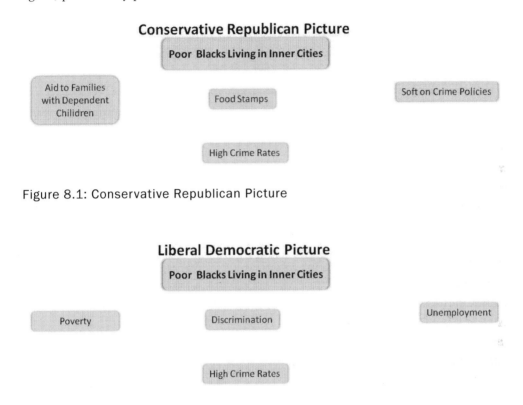

Figure 8.1: Conservative Republican Picture

Figure 8.2: Liberal Democratic Picture

CONSERVATIVE VICTORY AND ITS CONSEQUENCES

Conservatives and the Republican Party won this conflict and dominated American politics from 1980 until at least 2006, when that dominance was once again challenged. Alexander maintains that this is in accordance with her historical narrative. "Just as race had been used at the turn of the century by Southern elites to rupture class solidarity at the bottom of the income ladder, race as a national issue had broken up the Democratic New Deal bottom up coalition—a coalition dependent on substantial support from all voters, white and black at or below the median income" (Alexander 2012, 47).

Republicans, led by Ronald Reagan, used getting tough on crime and attacks on welfare as tacit attacks on poor African Americans designed to appeal to working-class and poor whites.

> To great effect Reagan echoed white frustration in race neutral terms through implicit racial appeals. His "colorblind" rhetoric on crime, taxes, and states' rights was clearly understood by white (and black) voters as having a racial dimension, though claims to that effect were impossible to prove. (48)

THE WAR ON DRUGS

In October 1982, President Reagan announced his War on Drugs. At the time, Alexander points out, less than 2 percent of Americans viewed drugs as the number one problem facing the country. This made little difference to Reagan, according to Alexander, because the War on Drugs was never about drugs. "The drug war from the onset had little to do with public concern about drugs and much to do with public concern about race. By waging a war on drug users and dealers, Reagan made good on his promise to crack down on the racially defined 'others'—the undeserving"

Figure 8.3: Ronald Reagan

(Alexander 2012, 49). Nor, Alexander points out, was Reagan's War on Drugs a response to the spread of crack cocaine into poor, urban, black communities. This occurred in 1985, several years after Reagan's announcement of the War on Drugs. The War on Drugs and the significant federal resources to fund it came before crack cocaine. Alexander doesn't minimize the negative effects of crack cocaine on black, inner-city communities. She rather connects it to rising unemployment in black inner-city communities. In her view, rising unemployment increased the incentive to sell drugs. She adds that there were other ways to deal with drug abuse and addiction—drug treatment, prevention, education, and economic investment in crime ridden communities (51). The reasons we chose a War on Drugs, she argues, were "traceable largely to racial politics and fear mongering. ... Conservatives found they could finally justify an all-out war on an 'enemy' that had been racially defined years before" (52).

CRIMINAL JUSTICE AS A SYSTEM OF RACIAL CONTROL

To make her case that the real enemy of the War on Drugs was black people, and that its aim was the construction of a new form of racialized caste appropriate to an era of colorblindness, Alexander constructs a picture of the American criminal justice system and how it works. She tries to establish that the astounding increase in the American prison population is the result of the incarceration of minor drug offenders, not violent career criminals. She says that the War on Drugs transformed the criminal justice system in ways that resulted in its control over a significant number of people, not because of their criminal behavior, but because of their status as poor and black. Finally, she argues that mass incarceration placed poor, young, black men in conditions that meet her definition of racialized caste. As an attorney and professor of law, Alexander is in a unique position to paint such a picture. The effectiveness with which she has done so no doubt accounts for the extraordinary popularity and influence of her book.

The War on Drugs and the Increase in Police Powers

Figure 8.4: San Francisco March 2016

Between 1980 and 2007 the number of those imprisoned in the United States rose from three hundred thousand to two million. If those on probation and parole are counted, the total rises to seven million. The vast majority of those imprisoned over the past twenty-five years has been imprisoned for drug-related crimes not involving violence. Possession of marijuana accounted for 80 percent of the growth in drug arrests in the 1990s. Alexander attributes the bulk of this increase not to an increase in crime, but to changes in the criminal justice system produced by the War on Drugs. The laws, policies, and funding provided through the War on Drugs fundamentally changed the way police, prosecutors, and judges behaved. Supreme Court decisions consistently affirmed the constitutionality of these changes.

Felons as the New Untouchables

Those who plead guilty to even minor drug offenses in exchange for reduced sentences or probation are still classified as felons. Because most job applications have a box requiring applicants to admit if they have ever been convicted of a felony, their employment possibilities are extremely limited. They cannot live in public housing, receive other forms of government assistance, qualify for student loans or, in some states, vote. It is for these reasons that Alexander argues that those labeled felons are consigned to undercaste status (Alexander 2012, 96).

> People who have been convicted of felonies almost never truly reenter the society they inhabited prior to their conviction. Instead, they enter a separate society, a world hidden from public view, governed by a set of oppressive and discriminatory rules and laws that do not apply to everyone else. They become members of an undercaste—an enormous population of predominantly black and brown people, who because of the drug war are denied basic rights and privileges of American citizenship and are permanently relegated to an inferior status. (187)

Mass Incarceration as the New Jim Crow

To make her case for mass incarceration as a new form of racialized caste, Alexander must make the case not only that convicted felons are consigned to a lifetime of

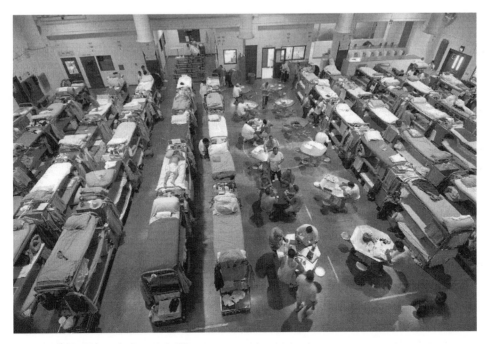

Figure 8.5: Mass Incarceration

inferior status, she must make the case that their status is the result of race. To do so, Alexander presents data suggesting that the War on Drugs has been waged overwhelmingly against poor, young African American males. Between 1983 and 2000 the incarceration rate for African Americans increased by twenty-six times. They increased for whites as well, but by much less (eight times). Of those convicted of drug crimes during this period, 75 percent were African American. In seven states, 80 to 90 percent of people incarcerated were African American (Alexander 2012, 98–99).

Alexander tries to demonstrate that poor, young, black men aren't incarcerated because they use and sell drugs, but because they are black. She does this by presenting evidence that most drug users and dealers are not African American. She presents studies indicating that whites use illegal drugs as frequently as, or more frequently than, African Americans. "People of all races use and sell drugs at remarkably similar rates. If there are differences surveys suggest that white youth are more likely to engage in illegal drug dealing than people of color" (99). In a survey conducted in 2000, the National Institute of Drug Abuse "reported that white students used cocaine at seven times the rate of black students, used crack cocaine at eight times the rate of black students, and used heroin at seven times the rate of black students. Nearly the same percentage of white and black high school seniors used marijuana. The National Household Survey on Drug Abuse conducted in the same year reported that white youth aged 12–17 were more than a third more likely to have sold drugs than African American youth" (99).

Despite the evidence that black youth don't use or sell drugs with greater frequency than white youth, they are admitted to prison at thirteen times the rate of white men (100). In 2006, one in nine black men between the ages of 20 and 35 were behind bars (100).

Alexander's Historical Narrative

Alexander tries to explain the problems facing people of color, including the problems of crime and rising rates of incarceration, by creating a picture of what the United States looks like and how it works. She employs a conflict perspective; concepts of race, caste, and mass incarceration; and data collected from historians and others to construct a historical narrative in which the condition of African Americans is presented in terms of a recurring pattern. Coalitions of white elites construct a racialized caste in order to control and exploit African Americans. An interracial coalition of poor people successfully destroys the caste system and attempts to replace it with a more egalitarian system of social relations. White elites respond by dividing up the coalition of poor people through racial bribes, winning over a section of the white poor and constructing a new form of racialized caste. Slavery, Jim Crow segregation, and mass incarceration are presented as different forms of racialized caste constructed, overcome, and then reconstructed in a new form through this recurring process.

Given the pattern she has constructed, it makes sense that Alexander would urge the formation of a new interracial coalition of poor people to struggle against and defeat the white elites who constructed mass incarceration as the new form of racialized caste. This time, Alexander hopes, the coalition of poor people will succeed not just in dismantling the latest form of racial caste, but in creating a more egalitarian social order as well. That, in her view, is the only way of preventing white elites from constructing a new form of racial caste to replace mass incarceration.

Structure of Alexander's Historical Narrative

Planter Elite divides poor by race
Slavery
Abolitionist Movement
Reconstruction (potential union of Poor Blacks and Whites)
Elite Reaction
Jim Crow (divides Poor Whites and Blacks)
Civil Rights Movement
Poor Peoples Movement (potential unity of poor Blacks and Whites against Wealthy Elites)
Elite Reaction
War on Drugs and Crime
Mass Incarceration and New Jim Crow
?

Figure 8.6: The Structure of Alexander's Narrative

THEORIZING IN ALEXANDER'S *THE NEW JIM CROW*: EVALUATION

What are we to make of the historical narrative that Alexander has constructed? First, we need to keep in mind that her narrative is something she has constructed to make sense of a part of American history; it is not an image of history itself. History is a collection of past documents and artifacts that historians have managed to find and archive. Historians puzzle over the contents of these archives and try to make some sense of them. On that basis, they try to figure out what happened in the past. Some historians and most social analysts try to go further, to develop explanations of why things happened the way that they did. One kind of historical explanation (not the only one) is a narrative explanation. Such narrative explanations are attempts to select and chronologically order some of these documents so that they form a coherent story—with a beginning, middle, and end, or a beginning, a complication, and a resolution. These historical narratives are attempts to explain what happened in the past and connect the explanation of past events to an account of what is happening in the present. Alexander's narrative is her attempt to provide this kind of explanation.

ALEXANDER'S HISTORICAL NARRATIVE: GIVING THE PRESENT ITS PAST

How good is her explanation? How should we evaluate it? First, we need to keep in mind the problem Alexander is attempting to address by constructing her narrative. She isn't trying to give the past its present as an historian might. She is trying to give the present its past. She is trying to explain the mass incarceration of poor, young, African American men. Her explanation is that mass incarceration is the latest form of racialized caste to which African Americans have been subjected in their history. Who is she offering this explanation to, and why? She makes this clear in the preface to *The New Jim Crow*. Her study is directed at people who are committed to racial justice but who underestimate the importance of mass incarceration in black communities.

What she seems to be trying to say to people like this is that the current mass incarceration of poor, young, black men is a problem for African Americans at a level of significance that parallels that of slavery and Jim Crow segregation. She also seems to be arguing that, just as it took mass interracial social movements to end slavery and Jim Crow, it will take a mass interracial social movement to end mass incarceration. Finally, she wants to argue that if people concerned about social justice don't want a new form of racial oppression to replace mass incarceration the way Jim Crow replaced slavery, this interracial social movement will have to do more than end mass incarceration; it will have to transform the United States into an egalitarian democracy.

She constructs a concept of racialized caste to make this argument to this audience. The concept is important because she uses it to connect slavery and Jim Crow to mass incarceration. In a sense, she is saying that if these are different forms of the same thing, then the dismantling of mass incarceration is as important as were the abolition of slavery and the ending of Jim Crow segregation. Because I largely share Alexander's ideological perspective, I want to try to be objective by being as tough in my evaluation of her theorizing as I can.

Narrative Coherence and Strength of Argument

One of the ways to evaluate a narrative explanation is on the basis of the coherence of the narrative. Does Alexander succeed in arguing that slavery, Jim Crow, and mass incarceration are different forms of the same thing? While some analysts distinguish slavery and caste as different forms of social stratification, seeing them both as forms of caste doesn't seem to me to discredit Alexander's narrative. She is on strong ground in conceiving of Jim Crow as a caste system. Nor is she alone in doing so (see Cox 1959; Dollard 1949).

The key to her argument, and its most controversial part, is her claim that mass incarceration is a new form of racialized caste deliberately constructed by segregationists to replace Jim Crow. I find this the least convincing and most confusing part of her argument.

Even if, as Alexander indicates, most segregationists favored getting tough on crime, it doesn't necessarily follow that most people who wanted to get tough on crime were segregationists. Indeed, as Alexander says, some black activists favored getting tough on crime. They may have been, as she suggests, "misguided," but they weren't segregationists. Her argument is further weakened by her claim that when people say they favor getting tough on crime, they really mean to establish a new form of racialized caste. As she admits, proving that when people say one thing they really mean something else is extremely difficult.

It is almost certainly true that this law-and-order rhetoric "proved highly effective in appealing to poor and working-class whites, particularly in the South, who were opposed to integration and frustrated by the Democratic party's apparent support for the Civil Rights Movement" (Alexander 2012, 43). However, it is also true that if the appeal of law-and-order rhetoric was limited to this grouping, it could not have succeeded in achieving "a major realignment of political parties in the United States" (43).

Political Parties

Another thing that I think weakens Alexander's theorizing is the absence of any real discussion of the role of political parties in the construction and dismantling of her racial castes. The splitting of the Democratic Party into Northern and Southern wings and the birth of radical antislavery republicanism is what led to the election of Lincoln as president and thus indirectly to the Civil War, the abolition of slavery, and Reconstruction. The professionalization of the late-nineteenth-century Republican Party and its transformation into a bureaucratic entity dedicated to winning elections and securing political offices as ends in themselves is crucial to the end of Reconstruction and the subsequent rise of Jim Crow segregation.

Most importantly, Alexander's failure to deal with the complexities involved in the resurgence of the Republican Party in the 1980s contributes to her failure to explain the political role of the wars on crime and drugs in the emergence of the Republican majority. Clearly, race and racism played an important role in the formation of the new Republican majority. But electoral majorities are constructed through coalitions. Former or covert segregationists were only part of that coalition. They couldn't have done what Alexander attributes to them on their own.

Is Affirmative Action a Racial Bribe?

Alexander seems to sense, but never successfully articulates, the effect of a "circulation of elites" and the "Iron Law of Oligarchy" (Michels, 1915) on the civil rights movement itself. She denounces affirmative action as a racial bribe and points correctly, I think, to the difficulty the policy raises for attracting poor whites into the interracial social movement she sees as the solution to the social problem she is addressing. What doesn't fit into Alexander's narrative is the role the end of Jim Crow segregation and the adoption of affirmative action policies played in removing some of the most talented and able members of the black community from that community. They have become members of the new professional, upper-middle class described by Murray. They have also become increasingly separated from the inner-city African American poor. That the leadership of the civil rights movement has itself become professionalized and more concerned with black upper-middle-class professionals like themselves than the inner city black poor should come as no surprise.

This is crucial, not only to Alexander's argument, but to the audience to which she addresses it. How did conservatives manage to take control of the Republican Party? How were they able to build a coalition strong enough not just to defeat the Democratic Party but to defuse movements for social and racial justice as well? This, I think, is what Alexander's audience needs to know if they are to successfully construct the new interracial movement for social justice she calls for.

CONCLUSION

What have we learned about the theorizing that goes into studies like Charles Murray's *Coming Apart* and Michelle Alexander's *The New Jim Crow*? For one thing, we should have learned that while it's important to learn the basic definitions of theoretical concepts, it's just as important to learn how these concepts are used in social studies. Culture, class, and caste look different when they are used to make arguments than they do when they are defined in texts. So do consensus and conflict perspectives. The theorizing that underlies good social studies employs both consensus and conflict. Theorizing that emphasizes consensus can't ignore social conflicts; and theorizing that emphasizes conflict can't ignore consensus. For Murray, consensus takes the form of a civic culture that is widely shared by most people in society. Murray is as interested in the forces that threaten that consensus as he is in what holds it together. Alexander is interested in conflict and the groups that wage it. She is also interested in the results of these conflicts. Eventually, the winners of these conflicts are able to use their victories to establish an uneasy and temporary consensus.

We should also have learned that point of view and audience are crucial parts of social theorizing and social inquiry. Charles Murray believes that the upper class should rule and that the lower and working classes should virtuously accept that rule and take pride in their own lot. Alexander believes that the poor and working classes should reject their lot, overcome their differences, and unite in a social movement that contests the power of wealthy elites. In the end, where you stand, who you stand with, and what you stand for makes a difference.

STUDY QUESTIONS

1. I have argued that often the theorizing done by social analysts is a "theorizing of the theorizing" done by social actors in their everyday lives. Describe liberal and conservative theorizing on the causes of the rise and decline of crime rates in the United States over the last fifty years.
2. How do sociology texts distinguish between consensus and conflict perspectives? Which perspective do Murray and Alexander take? How does the use of their perspective differ from the account of perspectives given in Wikipedia?
3. How does the ideological stance adopted by Murray and Alexander influence their theorizing?

ASSIGNMENT

1. What major concepts, data, and methods do you intend to use in your project?

SUGGESTED FURTHER READINGS

Alexander, Michelle. 2012. *The New Jim Crow: Mass Incarceration in the Age of Colorblindness*, rev. ed., 178–221 (The New Jim Crow). New York: The New Press.

Danto, Arthur. 1965. *Analytical Philosophy of History*, 233–57 (Historical Explanation: The Role of Narratives). Cambridge: Cambridge University Press.

Navy Vet Terp. August, 19, 2013. "The Emerging Republican Majority 44 Years Later." *Daily Kos*.

"Thirty Years of America's Drug War." *Frontline*. Public Broadcasting System. http://www.pbs.org/wgbh/pages/frontline/shows/drugs/cron/.

Weaver, Warren, Jr. 1969. "The Emerging Republican Majority." *The New York Times*, September 21.

IMAGE CREDITS

CHAPTER 9

ALISON WOLF'S *THE XX FACTOR: HOW THE RISE OF WORKING WOMEN HAS CREATED A FAR LESS EQUAL WORLD*

ESCAPING THE GENDERED CASTE, PART I: RATIONAL CHOICES AND UNINTENDED CONSEQUENCES

Wolf's topic is gender. She uses the concept of class as did Murray in *Coming Apart*. She also uses a conception of caste as did Alexander, though hers is gendered rather than racialized. Wolf is less directly ideological than both Murray and Alexander. Her passion is more muted, but it's there. She seems particularly passionate about the need to question the commonsense knowledge we have about the condition of women in the modern world and the effects of the feminist movement of the 1960s and 1970s.

OBJECT OF KNOWLEDGE: DEVELOPED SOCIETIES

Wolf concentrates on more or less the same time period as Murray and Alexander (the 1960s to the present). Her study, like theirs, has a historical dimension. Like Murray, she employs a historical zero point (1802, the year Jane Austen broke off her engagement). Instead of focusing on one society, however, Wolfe focuses on a kind of society. There are different terms for this kind of society—modern, industrial, developed. To be consistent, I will use the term developed to refer to societies that fit within this category. Western and northern European countries, Japan, South Korea, Canada, the United States, Australia, and New Zealand are usually classified as developed. While Wolf notes some differences between developed societies, by grouping them all together she is making the implicit assumption that they are, in important ways, including the ways she will study, very much the same. In other words, she uses "developed society" as a theoretical concept.

Figure 9.1: Jane Austen

USING CURIOSITIES, CONCERNS, PASSIONS, AND SOCIOLOGICAL IMAGINATION TO TRANSFORM A TOPIC INTO A PROBLEM

Wolf, like Murray and Alexander, uses curiosity, concern, passion, and sociological imagination to transform her topic into a social problem. Her study begins with curiosity and concern about people like herself, women from upper-middle-class English families who came of age in the 1970s. She is able to connect "people like her" to similar kinds of people in similar kinds of societies. Though she wasn't aware of it at the time, she sees women of her generation, growing up in countries like hers (developed societies), as having been a "hinge generation" whose lives changed how some women in developed societies live and work, changing these societies in fundamental ways in the process. The most important of these changes is increasing social inequality. This, for Wolf, is the problem.

KEY CONCEPTS: INSTRUMENTAL AND VALUE RATIONALITY

Like Weber, Wolf assumes that the people she studies are rational actors. Faced with alternatives they, as she puts it, "do their sums"—they weigh the costs and benefits of each alternative and make their choices by calculating the difference between these costs and benefits. When faced with alternatives that differ little in terms of cost-benefit ratios, people make choices based on individual preferences, what Wolf refers to as taste. In the aggregate, however, Wolf argues that when we look at millions of such choices, people doing their sums tend to cancel out individual tastes and preferences. This, for example, is how Wolf makes sense of women's decisions on whether or not to work outside the home. "At some level, consciously or unconsciously, we are all asking ourselves the same questions. Are there jobs around that are profitable? How much do I need the money? What will I lose if I trade in paid hours for unpaid? The workplace and home mean more or less to different people, because people have different priorities. But across the world the equation comes out differently, on average, for particular groups" (Wolf 2013, 20). Well-educated professional women in the upper-middle class decide differently than other women with other backgrounds.

Note the difference between how Wolf explains different behaviors of people at different income levels with how Murray does. Murray attributes the differences in behavior between people in his new upper class and his new lower class to differences in values, to the presence or absence of virtue. Wolf, by contrast, argues that both groups do their sums. If the behavior of members of one group differs from that of the other, it's because the sums come out differently for members of each group. This kind of opportunity cost thinking and action is what Max Weber (1978, 25) called instrumental rationality, which he distinguished from value rationality—"a conscious belief in the value for its own sake of some ethical, religious or other form of behavior, independently of its prospects for success." As we will see below, Wolf does however make the point that it is a particular kind of value rationality that provided the historical context for the kind of instrumental rationality that has become dominant among people generally in developed societies.

Prior to 1960 (Murray's zero point), educated upper-middle-class women demonstrated what Murray would call their virtue by taking part in volunteer and charity work. Educated women went into teaching not just because it was the only profession open to them but because they saw teaching as a calling and a vocation. "Early female educators, in schools and universities, lived and breathed a moral seriousness that is far removed from anything in elite education today. They were not chafing against the constraints of an occupation they were forced and doomed to follow. For many of them, teaching was a vocation and a calling" (Wolf, 2013, 135).

Wolf uses the same value rationality to explain why top universities run and staffed by men let women in. Wolf says it wasn't a matter of self-interest or instrumental rationality, at least not at first. It was the post–World War II advance of egalitarian and democratic values. "By the 1960s, the same changing values that fueled feminism, spread universal suffrage and demanded meritocracy in the labor market had been adopted by university leaders. They found it increasingly difficult to justify or believe in anything other than gender-blind admissions policies" (Wolf 2013, 107).

Wolf maintains that value rationality also accounts for some of the increasing contributions of men to unpaid labor in the home. She argues that, contrary to what most of us think, there is more sharing of unpaid labor in the home than there once was, though women still do the majority of it. Value rationality plays a role in this change, Wolf argues. "Shifts in power, reflecting shifts in earnings and the labor market, must be one reason why men are doing more at home and why total hours worked have equalized. But is that all there is? Surely values matter as well" (73). "Ideas about what is fair and right seem genuinely to have changed, so that the vast majority of men in developed countries feel that they ought to do their 'fair share' of household work and childcare" (74).

THE MOVE FROM VIRTUE TO INSTRUMENTAL RATIONALITY

Still, Wolf sees, as Weber did, a general movement toward instrumental rationality in developed societies. Unlike Murray, Wolf sees the accompanying decline of value rationality (virtue) in the past fifty years not as limited to the new lower class in America, but as characteristic of most people in developed societies.

According to Wolf, it was primarily among upper- and upper-middle-class women that the virtues of service and religiously based volunteerism (value rationality) once flourished; and it is this group that has "moved furthest away from life focused on church and religion" (Wolf 2013, 145). Partially as a result, the volunteerism that thrived between 1860 and 1960 has all but disappeared. If Wolf is right, then Murray's claim that the American upper-middle class still largely practices the founding virtues should be viewed with skepticism (he presents little evidence to back up this claim). It is likely they are "doing their sums" and practicing instrumental rationality, just like almost everybody else in the developed world.

According to Wolf, it is instrumental rationality that is at the center of contemporary culture, not just in the United States but across the developed world. If she is right about this, then it is not the absence of shared values that threatens to tear such societies apart. It is the way those particular values, when carried out systematically on a very wide scale, work themselves out that threatens to lead developed societies to come apart.

UNINTENDED CONSEQUENCES: THE RISE OF UPPER-MIDDLE-CLASS PROFESSIONAL WOMEN AND THE RISE IN INEQUALITY

Wolf concentrates her attention on one particular form of this coming apart—the separation of well-educated, upper-middle-class professional women from other women. Wolf argues that prior to the 1970s it made sense to talk about women, the lives of women, and women's choices. It was possible in fundamental ways to think of women as the same. Women formed a caste that was separate from men, that dictated what they could and could not do, and how they could and could not live their lives. Prior to 1970, the lives of all women were centered on marriage and children. The life chances of all women, regardless of class, were determined by whom they married. Their lives were centered on taking care of the house, tending to the needs of their husbands, and raising their children.

THE HINGE GENERATION: BREAKING OUT OF THE FEMININE CASTE

Wolf argues that for the first time in history her "hinge generation" of women broke out of this feminine caste. They went to university as many of their mothers did. They went on to graduate school as very few of their mothers did. Then they went on to have careers outside the home, working in well-paid professions alongside (and above) men with backgrounds and educations much like theirs. When (and if) they married, when (and if) they had children, they went right on working. They began to live lives much like that of the men in their class. Their lives ceased to be centered on marriage and child-rearing and became centered instead (mostly though not exclusively) on their work. Wolf tries to show that succeeding generations of women like hers are likely to do the same, reinforcing and extending social inequality in the process.

A Different Kind of Woman

According to Wolf, well-educated, upper-middle-class professional women now number approximately 70 million (around a fifth of all women globally fit into this category, most concentrated in developed countries)). She says that for the other 80 percent of women, life continues to go on pretty much as it always has. Their lives are defined by their gender. Even in developed societies, most women work in gender-specific occupations where they do what has traditionally been considered women's work. They leave the workplace when they have children and stay out of it as long as they can. When they return to work, they prefer to work part time. They put family and children first and work a distant second.

Wolf's study is largely about the lives of these new, well-educated, upper-middle-class professional women. She tries to establish connections between the professional life of these women and other aspects of their lives. She then attempts to show how their lives as a whole distance them from other women and contribute to growing social inequality.

As we have already seen, there are a number of ways to conceptualize, categorize, and compare "kinds" of people. We can group people by gender, race, ethnicity, by country, by kind of country, by income or socioeconomic status. We can compare the lives of people living now with the lives of people living in different historical periods. In *The XX Factor*, Wolf concentrates her attention on a particular grouping of women in a particular type of society. She concentrates on highly educated,

Figure 9.2: Professional Woman

well-paid professional women in developed societies. Her most frequent point of comparison is this grouping of women with other women in developed societies. She also looks at the historical development of this group of women. She compares how women in developed societies live now with how they lived in earlier periods. She sometimes compares the position of women in developed societies with the position of women in developing and underdeveloped societies. Occasionally, she compares women with men. However, these latter comparisons are secondary to Wolf's study. They provide context for her primary point of comparison, that between the 20 percent of women in developed societies who are well educated and work in well-paid professions, and the other 80 percent of women in such societies who are far less well educated and less well paid.

COGNITIVE ELITE

Wolf's women are part of Murray's new upper-middle class—not his broad elite (the top 5 percent) or his narrow elite (the top 1 percent), but part of the 20 percent from which these narrow and broad elites are drawn. Wolf, unlike Murray, doesn't claim these women are innately smarter than others, but they are, for the most part, symbolic analysts and in that sense part of the cognitive elite. They work as managers, administrators, attorneys, bankers, professors, executives, journalists, and consultants. There are as yet comparatively fewer women engineers, but Wolf is convinced that will soon change. Wolf agrees with Murray's observation that the new economy is ideally suited to their talents and that they are rewarded accordingly.

EDUCATION

Like Murray, Wolf recognizes that modern professional elites are formed in top universities. She emphasizes, as Murray did not, that "modern higher education is serving women very well indeed" (Wolf 2013, 90). Over the last forty years, gender discrimination in elite colleges has diminished. Once elite schools dropped "separate but equal" women's colleges for co-education, women quickly reached parity with males in top schools around the world. "The Ivy League colleges, so recently all male, now have a small majority of female over male undergraduates" (102). In 1970, only 10 percent of the undergraduate student body at Oxford and Cambridge was female. Today they account for nearly half. The same is true of the prestigious Grandes Ecoles in France. "Even in Japan, that bastion of male elites, the University of Tokyo aims and expects 30 percent of its students to be female in the very near future" (103). What is true of undergraduate schools is even truer of graduate and professional schools. Almost 60 percent of medical students in the United Kingdom are female. In the United States, almost half of medical students are female. All over the developed world, law schools have a majority of female students (93).

This has been tough on men. While the number of college graduates has exploded over the past forty years, the number of openings at elite schools has not. The number of men attending Ivy League schools is the same today as it was in 1950. "Thousands of young men who would have had an Ivy League undergraduate education in the old all-male days now don't and won't. Many thousands of women have taken their place" (103).

SOCIAL CAPITAL

The reason graduates of elite schools do so well in their future careers is not just because of the education they receive. It also because of the social capital they acquire. It is the contacts they make; it's the networking they do. "Now increasingly it's women as well as men drinking beer as freshm[e]n; women and men working together in the academic pressure cooker of a final year; and women as well as men calling men and other women on behalf of alumni networks" (Wolf 2013, 104).

As women have become an ever-larger presence on elite college campuses, employers who recruit from these campuses have increased the number of women they recruit. Just as the number of openings at top universities is limited, so is the number of top firms and top jobs at those firms. "If women couldn't be CEOs, then some additional men would have had the chance to head Pearson, IBM, Pepsi, and Hewlett-Packard. If women couldn't be politicians, then men who have never made it into contemporary politics would be senators, MPs and ministers" (106).

THE GREAT COMPRESSION

Wolf indicates, as I suggested earlier, that the shared civic culture that defined Murray's United States at his zero point of 1960 may have been a product of what economists call the "Great Compression," which was characteristic of developed countries from the 1930s until the 1960s. During this period, the developed world was characterized by relative equality of income (at least compared to what preceded and followed this period). From the 1970s to the present, income inequality has consistently grown throughout the developed world, separating the upper and the

Social Capital

Like all concepts, the meaning of "social capital" is dependent upon the use to which it is put. In general it refers to the social value of our relationship with others—the networks we are part of, the friendships we have and the organizations to which we belong. Our social capital is productive in the sense that we can use it to accomplish things we might not be able to without it. It also gives credit we can call on when we need it.

Figure 9.3: Social Capital

upper-middle class from everybody else. Women's wages have increased considerably during the post–Great Compression period, while men's wages have stayed the same or gone down (though this, as with the concept of "women" and "men," may be less useful than it seems). The lion's share of this increase hasn't gone to women working in childcare or at Wal-Mart. It has gone to well-educated, upper-middle-class professional women. Thus, Wolf argues, the growth in income inequality hasn't just separated the rich from everybody else. It has separated the top 20 percent of female earners from the other 80 percent of female earners (119).

PATTERN OF CONNECTIONS

Wolf constructs a picture of the social life of this new group of highly educated women by connecting their position in the labor market to other aspects of their

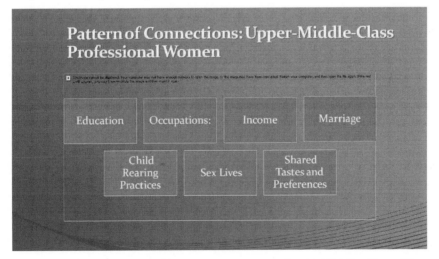

Figure 9.4: Pattern of Connections: Contemporary Upper-Middle-Class Women

lives, and then contrasting their lives with those of other women. She connects work life to sex life; marriage patterns; fertility rates; child-rearing practices; and home life and leisure activities. She also tries to show how these connections tend to reproduce themselves over generations, increasing social and economic inequality in developed societies in the process.

We will examine how she makes these connections and separations in the next chapter.

STUDY QUESTIONS

1. What does Wolf mean by the concept of the hinge generation, and how does she use it in her study?
2. What does Wolf mean by "doing their sums?"
3. How does Wolf use the concepts of instrumental rationality and value rationality in her study? Give an example of how she uses each.
4. What does Wolf mean by feminine caste? How does she use this concept in her study?
5. Compare Wolf's use of the concept of class with Murray's.
6. What is meant by the Great Compression?
7. How, according to Wolf, has the rise of well-educated, upper-middle-class women contributed to economic and social inequality?
8. What aspects of social life of does Wolf connect to design the picture of social life she uses to address her social problem?

ASSIGNMENTS

1. Do the reading(s) you are analyzing distinguish between the forms of rationality employed by the social actors in the study? Give an example of the use of this distinction in the reading(s).
2. Do you envision using the distinction between forms of rationality in your research proposal?
3. What unit of analysis will you use in the research project you are proposing, and why?

Suggested Further Readings

Merton, Robert K. 1936. "The Unanticipated Consequences of Purposive Social Action." *American Sociological Review* 1 (6): 895.

Weber, Max. 1978. *Economy and Society*, Volume One, edited by Guenther Roth and Claus Wittich, 4–24 (Types of Social Action). Berkeley: University of California Press.

Image Credits

CHAPTER 10

ALISON WOLF'S *THE XX FACTOR: HOW THE RISE OF WORKING WOMEN HAS CREATED A FAR LESS EQUAL WORLD*

LIFESTYLES OF THE WELL-OFF, PART II

Sex Life

The sex lives of all women changed dramatically when safe, reliable birth control became widely available (Wolf, 2013, 152). Prior to that, "female sex happened overwhelmingly after (as well as mostly within) marriage. Outside of marriage "pregnancy was more likely to be a prelude to a shotgun marriage than to an illegitimate child; but if the man couldn't be persuaded or forced to do the 'right thing,' then women faced social ruin, and their babies, for the most part, a miserable fate. With the Pill, everything changed" (Wolf 2013, 152).

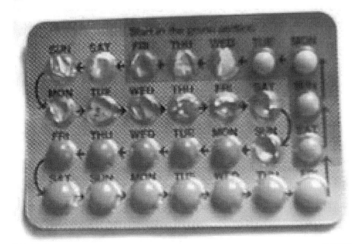

Figure 10.1: Birth Control

For the first time in history, women were able to have sex with the confidence that they wouldn't get pregnant. Wolf cites studies estimating that only 6 percent of American teenagers engaged in premarital sex in 1960. Today, three-fourths of American and British teenagers are sexually active. "Among young women in their twenties and thirties fewer than one in 10 reported going without sex in the previous year. ... We are looking at sea change in behavior" (153).

While the pill has changed the sexual behavior of all women, it has changed the sexual behavior of well-educated and less-educated women differently. Wolf attributes this to the very different opportunities offered to women in the top 20 percent compared to the 80 percent below them (153).

Wolf pictures women's sexual decision making in starkly instrumental terms. "Heterosexual sex is something that only women can give to men, and heterosexual sex is something that men, really, badly want ... women have historically squeezed everything they can out of this ... sex proffered, sex withheld were the main assets that girls possessed, and the one on which, for the overwhelming majority of men, they had a monopoly" (155).

THE SEX LIVES OF THE TOP 20 PERCENT AND THE OTHER 80 PERCENT DIFFER

In the post-pill era, attractiveness still matters, but it matters differently and differently to the top 20 percent than it does to other women. As a result, the sexual behavior of these two groups now differs. While the sexual revolution hit college campuses first in the late 1960s, by the 1990s the sexual habits of young women had changed. Today, sex prior to the age of 16 is far more common among girls who don't plan to go to college than those who do (Wolf 2013, 161). Women graduates, perhaps because they start having sex later, report having fewer sex partners. By the time they reach their 30s, graduates have caught up or even passed non-graduates in their number of sex partners (165).

More-educated and less-educated women differ in their attitudes toward what kind of sex lives people "should" have. Charles Murray might be surprised at these differences. Well-educated women are more tolerant of sexual promiscuity than are the less educated. Well-educated women are more tolerant of homosexuality than the less educated. While most women say they are satisfied with their sex lives, younger, non-graduate women are not. Well-educated women would like to have more sex; less well-educated women, less (172).

EROTIC CAPITAL

Sex appeal is still important to women. Wolf cites sociologist Catherine Hakim's argument that because men are more interested in sex than women, women have more "erotic capital" (190). Wolf employs the law of supply and demand to explain sexual relations as well as other kinds of relationships. "Male sexuality has little value, because there is more of it on offer than women want: the reverse is not true and this 'gives women the upper hand in sexual bargaining and private relationships'" (190). Wolf argues that this surplus of erotic capital is an asset for attractive, well-educated professional women, and many use it to get a competitive advantage at work. Evidence shows it is particularly valuable in sales and fund-raising (191–92). Wolf adds that attractive female professionals have to be careful how they use their attractiveness. They need to be "charming" but not "flirty" (193).

MARRIAGE AND CHILDREN

These highly educated, well-paid professional women have tended to marry highly educated, well-paid professional men. They have tended to get married later than women have in the past (in their late 20s or early 30s) and they have tended to have fewer children. The drastic lowering of fertility rates in developed countries is an increasing concern of their governments. Fertility rates in America are dropping for all women, but for highly educated women most of all. Before 1970 every educational group was more than reproducing itself. Now, only the least educated are. "It is amongst the educated that fertility has dropped furthest and fastest" (28). In Europe, fertility rates vary by country and are affected by government policy. "Fertility is higher in Scandinavia, with its large number of public sector jobs for women, backed by very generous parental leave, and lower in southern Europe with far fewer benefits for single and working mothers." But government policies aimed directly at raising fertility rates have had only modest effects. France has spent a lot of money in an effort to increase fertility rates with only modest effects. "Governments would have to spend a great deal of money to increase birth rates substantially among the professional classes" (40).

So, while family size is shrinking generally in most developed countries, that of well-educated professionals has shrunk the fastest. Less-educated women have their children far earlier, on average, than do graduates; but most do not, today, have more than two. In most countries, graduate women are more likely than others to have one child than two. They are more likely to be childless and much less likely to be in the small minority who still has more than three (39).

CHILDREN: FEWER, LATER FOR THE TOP 20 PERCENT

Wolf suggests that well-educated professional women have fewer children later in life largely for instrumental reasons. Today's professional women plan to have their first child much later than did previous generations. In 1970, having a first child after the age of 20 was highly unusual for any class. Today, in the developed world, 30 to 35 is peak child-bearing age for female professionals (Wolf 2013, 34). Childlessness is an unintended consequence of those instrumentally rational decisions. While most professional women would like to have children, preferably two, by putting off child bearing until their 30s or later, they often find they can't. Wolf says that while we hear a lot about women who have their first child in their late 30s or early 40s, we hear a lot less about the far greater number of women who try to have children at this age and fail (41).

The age at which the other 80 percent of women have children is much younger. In the United States, four out of five women who don't complete high school are mothers by the age of 25. In Britain about half of the women who don't complete secondary school have a child by the age of 22 (34). Again, Wolf argues that the age at which women have their first child is largely a matter of cost-benefit analysis. So, she says, is the decision to have a child outside of marriage.

She uses the analysis of Kathryn Edin and Maria Kefalas (2005) in *Promises I Can Keep: Why Poor Women Put Motherhood before Marriage* to make this point. This is an in-depth study of 162 poor, single mothers in the Philadelphia area. The study found that these women were overwhelmingly positive about motherhood. Wolf suggests that these women, like professional women, "do their sums" before making the decision to have a child. It's just that the sums come out very differently for the two groups. Poor, young women don't sacrifice rewarding careers by having a child when they are young and unmarried. Wolf argues that poor, young women with little education don't believe that delaying child bearing will have a major effect on their lives, and she suggests that their reasoning is sound. The same jobs that are available for unskilled women will be available no matter their age when they enter the job market (35–36).

THE UNINTENDED CONSEQUENCES OF GOVERNMENT POLICIES ON FERTILITY

Wolf argues that government policy contributes to the widening gap between the most- and least-educated women and their childbearing decisions. Murray argues that poor single mothers have less virtue than do women who delay having children until they are married, and that the decision to have children out of wedlock or not is a matter of value rationality. He also argues that welfare-state policy encourages the wrong values. Wolf argues that the decision to have a child and under what conditions is a matter of opportunity costs and instrumental rationality. She too, however, thinks that welfare- state policies make poor, young, unmarried women's desire to have a child make more instrumental sense. "Today ... in almost all developed societies single mothers, whether unmarried, separated, widowed or divorced, have a right to benefits. These may not offer an affluent life but they certainly offer a supportable one. And the fewer your prospects, the lower your earnings before you become a mother, the better life on benefits with a baby will look" (Wolf 2013, 37).

WOMEN, CLASS, FAMILY, AND WORK

Women have always worked, unless you don't consider housekeeping and child-rearing work. Until relatively recently, however, most women who worked outside the home left their jobs when they had a child. In the first half of the twentieth century, they rarely came back to the workforce. They stayed home and raised the children. By midcentury returning to the workforce became standard, but the time out of the workforce before they did so was around twelve years. There was little or no difference in terms of class. By the time postwar baby boomers became mothers, the time out of the workforce had dropped to six years. There was still no difference between classes (Wolf 2013, 44).

Today, there is a major class and educational difference in the time mothers stay out of the workforce after having a child. Most non-graduate new mothers still stay out of the workforce a good while, and when they return, try to find jobs that fit their work life around the family. They prefer to work part time. Highly educated professional women behave very differently. The most highly educated new mothers return to work the quickest—most highly educated women born after 1970 return to work within a year of giving birth (45). Again, Wolf attributes the difference between the groups to differing costs and opportunities. "Small children require a lot of care; someone has to look after them. If your baby sitters need to be paid, then you need to make enough to cover that. ... The lower-paying the jobs, the less financial sense it makes; and it is especially unlikely to make sense if you are eligible for state benefits" (47).

THE PROBLEM WITH AVERAGING WOMEN'S INCOME

Wolf argues that it is this time out of the workforce that accounts for much of the difference between the lifetime average earnings of women and men. "Multiple studies in the 1980s and 1990s all highlighted the way motherhood affected careers. On average mothers earned less; theirs was a story of interrupted employment and less success later on" (48). The well-educated, upper-middle-class professional woman who has a child is not average. The graduate mother today who delays having children until she is in her 30s and goes back to work full time within a year suffers little earning loss (49). Wolf argues that the difference in lifetime earnings between women and men is borne almost entirely by the other 80 percent of women. "Motherhood now typically 'costs' low earners much more, in terms of their life-time earnings and in comparison, with men, than it does the average graduate, because it is the lower earners who most often change their work lives" (49).

CHILD-REARING PRACTICES

Highly educated, professional women, like most parents, want their children to succeed. Their opportunities to help them do so are increased if they have their children later in life and return to full-time work quickly. Financially, it is important not to interrupt their careers when they have children. "They need to be earning enough, to be successful enough, to go back to work, to afford childcare, afford home help and still come out in profit" (54).

When well-educated, upper-middle-class professionals become mothers, they raise their children differently than do other mothers. Professional women can afford (though just barely) to rely more on formal childcare than others mothers can. This has resulted in what Wolf calls the rebirth of the servant classes. Domestic service was once a leading female profession. In 1870 at least half the women employed in America were domestic servants. On the eve of World War I, at least a third still was. By the early 1970s, sociologists were writing obituaries for domestic service.

The well-educated professional mother has brought it back. The most highly paid professional women can afford to have nannies to help with child-rearing. However, even for mothers in the top 20 percent, in-house nannies are prohibitively expensive. In the United States, they cost between $22,000 and $36,000 a year (Wolf 2013, 58). Only those professional women on the top end of the 20 percent of earners can afford them. The rest rely on fee-charging daycare nurseries. This, too, is very expensive. For children under the age of two in the United States, $1500 to $2,000 a month is not unusual (59).

THE GLOBAL CHILDCARE CHAIN

Increasingly, nannies and day nursery employees are from developing or underdeveloped countries, creating what Wolf calls a global care chain (59). In the United
States, care workers come from Mexico and Central America; in Greece, they come
from Sri Lanka; in other parts of Western Europe, they come from Poland (59).
Lower-income couples rely on informal childcare (babysitters), relatives, and tag-
team parenting. Parents who can't afford formal daycare have to try to juggle their
work shifts so that one parent watches the children while the other works (61).

HOME LIFE AND LEISURE TIME

Wolf employs time-use surveys to show that all women spend far less time at unpaid
labor around the house than they once did. Wolf says while this reduction has resulted in part from the widespread use of modern appliances—dishwashers, washing
and drying machines, and vacuums—much more of it results from the vast reduction
in time spent in cooking and food preparation. Cooking has gone commercial. Not
only are far more meals eaten outside the home, those eaten inside the home are increasingly prepared elsewhere—as frozen food, prepared meals, or take out. "Today,
even women with children at home average an hour a night on preparing food and
clearing up; for employed women it is just over half an hour" (66).

MORE MONEY, LESS LEISURE TIME

While there is less housework for everyone to do than there was forty years ago, most
people work fewer hours as well. In non-elite homes, free time is spent on leisure
including, as Murray suggests, sleeping and watching television (in his terms, "goof-
ing off"). In professional households, decreased housework has meant increased paid
work. In professional households, both men and women work more hours than they
did in the 1960s, some considerably more. They also sleep fewer hours and watch
less television than do nonprofessionals. As a result, Wolf calls the new professional
couple "time poor" (Wolf 2013, 80).

The couples that put the most time in at work, paid and unpaid, are those with
children under seven. Wolf says that professional couples spend more time at child-
rearing than do non-elite couples. "It is true for men and for women. And the gap
between them and other families is rising" (83). Wolf employs the findings of two
leading female experts to suggest that this difference between elite families and

others has a lot to do with investment. "If you've made it to the top yourself you'll do (almost) anything you can to stop your children sliding" (87).

THE SOLIDIFICATION OF THE UPPER-MIDDLE-CLASS FAMILY

While rates of illegitimacy are rising dramatically throughout the developed world, well-educated, upper-middle-class illegitimacy rates remain very low. "Everywhere the most affluent and educated mothers are the least likely to be single, whether it is in Seattle or Stockholm, Oslo or Ottawa" (216). According to Wolf, this isn't because well-educated, upper-middle-class professional women have a different sexual moral code than other women; it's because the opportunity cost ratio works out differently for them than for other women (217).

HAVING CHILDREN AND DOING YOUR SUMS

Highly educated, upper-middle-class professional women take a major risk when they have a child. They have a lot going for them and single parenthood on a limited income has little appeal to them. "Most successful women will therefore only have a baby given the clear commitment and financial assurance offered by marriage: marriage that is to someone at or close to their own educational and income level, who can help them raise a 'high quality' child and with whom their children will have full inheritance rights. No marriage, no baby" (219).

THE UPPER-MIDDLE-CLASS BUBBLE

As Murray suggested, contemporary upper-middle-class young people live their lives largely isolated from people unlike themselves. They are raised in upper-middle-class neighborhoods and attend elite colleges. However, these upper-middle-class women don't marry men who live in the neighborhood or even men they meet in college. They marry in their thirties and usually to men several years their senior. Usually, highly educated professional women marry men they meet at or through work.

Overwhelmingly, they tend to marry men like themselves—highly educated, successful, upper-middle-class or upper-class professionals. In the social studies literature, this is called "assortative marriage." When successful, highly educated women

Figure 10.2: Upper-Middle-Class Family

marry successful, highly educated men, they form households and raise families with very high incomes, and all the advantages and perks that come with that. That is why "when it comes to deciding society's winners, and its structure of power and wealth, it is parents and children who are the key players" (Wolf 2013, 231).

One route to success is through elite education and not just college education. Well-educated, upper-middle-class couples start their kids on the race to the top early. They work hard and spend serious money to get their children into the right preschool and high school, provide them with tutors and all the relevant extras to increase their chances of getting into an elite college. Wolf quotes Amy Wax, who notes that "getting your kid into Harvard or whatever is a full-time job. It's building the resume, taking the kids to activities, making sure they have the enrichment. You're doing everything for them. And you're afraid not to because if you just let them do it for themselves they'll screw up, and other parents are doing it for them" (245).

RUNNING THE FAMILY BUSINESS

The other path to the top is taking over the family business. Most of the world's businesses remain, as they always have been, family businesses. This is true not only in the United States but in developed societies as different as Germany and Sweden as well. Traditionally, the order of succession dictated that sons took over family businesses. It's not clear if that succession order still holds. Wolf says that it is impossible to know for sure but points to well-known examples from around the world in which major family businesses have been taken over by daughters. Ana Patricia

Botin is CEO of Santander in the UK; Georgia Rinehart is executive chairman of the HPPL mining giant (238). Women have taken charge of some unlikely businesses. Christie Hefner has taken over Playboy Enterprises from her father Hugh Hefner; Jim McMahon shares control of the family professional wrestling empire with his wife (158). As is now well known, Donald Trump's daughter not only has her own business, but plays a major role in her father's as well.

Across the developed world, upper-middle-class parents do whatever they can (which is a great deal) to see that their children stay on top. "The tendency for children born into the top fifth of the developed world to stay there is both high and surprisingly uniform. ... Among the elites, the family hasn't disintegrated as a result of women's new workplace opportunities. It has morphed into something as formidable as ever before" (249).

MAKING SENSE OF INEQUALITY AND MAKING SENSE OF IT DIFFERENTLY: EVALUATING THE THEORIZING IN *THE XX FACTOR*

Wolf's topic, like that of Murray, is inequality. Murray's and Wolf's differing curiosities, concerns, and passions led them to transform this topic into different problems, and to view them in starkly different terms. For Murray, the problem of inequality is that of the unraveling of shared culture in the United States. To illustrate his problem, Murray selects a zero point in the history of the United States, the symbolic date of November 3, 1963, and presents a picture of what the United States looked like at this point, when its shared culture remained intact. He then presents a picture of what "white America" looked like in 2010. He concentrates on white America to demonstrate that the cultural collapse of the new lower class was not a question of race or, in Alexander's terms, racialized caste, but one of class. The picture he presents of America in 2010 is one of a country with its shared culture coming apart along class lines. A new upper class has used its superior intellect and wealth to create a lifestyle that isolates it from the rest of the country; a new lower class has mired itself in a culture of poverty by shedding America's founding virtues of industry, honesty, religiosity, and a belief in the nuclear family. Murray's solution to the cultural coming apart of America is for the new upper class, which still possesses these virtues, to overcome its isolation and devote itself to spreading these values to the rest of the country, particularly to the new lower class. In other words, (and these are not his words) to act like a ruling class by making its values the values of American society at large.

INCREASING INEQUALITY: IN PART AN UNINTENDED CONSEQUENCE OF THE RISE OF WELL-EDUCATED PROFESSIONAL WOMEN

Wolf presents the problem of social inequality as, in part, an unintended consequence of the rise of a new group of well-educated, upper-middle-class professional women. She tries to show that these women have succeeded in breaking out of the feminine caste and separated themselves from other women in the process. They have become more or less equal partners with men of the same class. In doing so, they have contributed to the growing inequality between classes. While Wolf presents a picture depicting how this has happened, it's not clear to me that she shows how this problem might be addressed.

DEVELOPED SOCIETIES AND MODERNIZATION THEORY

Instead of focusing her attention on one society, Wolf focuses in on one kind of society—developed society. While I don't think it has a major effect on her picture of the countries she fits into this classification, it needs to be pointed out that "developed society" is a concept with a relatively long history going back to Durkheim, and has its share of critics. Developed society is a central concept in modernization theory. According to this theory, developed societies are modern societies with market economies and democratic nation-state governments that represent their citizens while respecting their human rights. This kind of society first developed in Western Europe, spread relatively quickly to the United States, Canada, and Australia, then, somewhat later, to Japan. According to modernization theorists, those societies which have yet to undergo the development process—underdeveloped societies—will eventually become more like developed societies. Those countries that are relatively far along on this process are classified as developing societies.

Wolf in large part embraces modernization theory in her analysis of developing societies, which she compares to developed societies at similar stages of development. She pictures these societies as "behind" developed societies, but moving faster than the first developed societies did because they have their examples to follow. Wolf assumes that developing societies will inevitably follow the lead of developed societies by adopting their values, including the value of equality between men and women.

> Most developing countries are far from achieving across-the-board equality between women and men. ... Yet in all the big and successful

developing countries of today—China, India, Muslim Indonesia—women play a significant role at the top of the job market, among the educated and well off. (Wolf 2013, 114)

Wolf believes that developing societies will inevitably adopt the ideas and values of developed societies.

Most contemporary nations sign up to a large number of common values and practices including political democracy. Here too there is overwhelming acceptance of equal access. Rich, poor, men and women, should all enjoy the same rights at the ballot box. ... In explaining the rapid progress of women in the developing world, the legitimacy of these values is crucially important, because it makes them impossible for leaders to ignore. And if women have an equal right to vote, if women have as much formal right to enter politics as men, then you set up a dynamic process that changes society. (116)

This is certainly what modernization theorists theorize, but they are not without their critics. Dependency theorists and world-system analysts argue that so-called developed countries and underdeveloped countries have been interconnected for a long time, and still are. They theorize that the development of some societies has been and is dependent on the underdevelopment of others. If they are right, then the world might well change very differently than Wolf foresees.

The deepening of the divide between classes in developed countries may be accompanied by an even deeper divide between rich and poor in developing and underdeveloped societies. That divide won't be lessened by the rise of well-educated, upper-middle-class professional women in these societies. Indeed, it may deepen that divide, as Wolf argues it has in developed societies. The existence of a global care chain through which poor women from the developing and underdeveloped world raise the children and clean the houses of the rich in the developed world isn't a promising sign.

Wolf sees elites in developing and underdeveloped countries as pursuing the same mix of instrumental and value rationality as have the elites in developed countries. They will mostly do their sums, calculate costs and opportunities, and act accordingly. But at key points their actions will be in accordance with certain values even if the sums don't add up. At key points their actions will be guided by egalitarian values, as were the male elites of top Western universities in the 1960s. Contemporary and future elites in the developing and underdeveloped world may well be guided by a mix of instrumental and value rationality in the future. It is far from certain that the mix will be the same in the future as it has been in the past.

INFERRING MOTIVES FROM BEHAVIOR

Indeed, it is far from clear that Wolf has definitively shown what the motives and reasons are for the actions of the people she studied. Most of the time, she infers the reasoning behind social actions from their results. This is particularly true when she focuses on women who are not in the group of well-educated, upper-middle-class professionals. In the case of the latter group, she uses her contacts to conduct interviews with professional women to ask them why they do what they do. She rarely does that with the other 80 percent of women. Time-use diaries can indicate what people do; they don't indicate why they do it. The only real exception to this is Wolf's use of Kathryn Edin and Maria Kefalas' study in *Promises I Can Keep: Why Poor Women Put Motherhood before Marriage* of poor, young, single mothers in Philadelphia. While it's an excellent study, it's a pretty slender reed on which to hang your account of why 80 percent of the women in the developed world do what they do.

BREAKING UP THE 80 PERCENT

In fairness to Wolf, I'm not sure there is a secure enough reed on which to hang such an account. Eighty percent of the women in the developed world may be too big a percentage to make much sense of. It needs to be broken up. When Wolf does break this 80 percent up, it's often to compare women who haven't completed secondary school with women who have graduated from elite colleges. Her picture of women in the developed world would have been more compelling had she compared women graduates of elite colleges with graduates of non-elite colleges, community colleges, and women with some college. Her analysis would be strengthened had she shown that these women remain confined to the female caste.

AMERICAN EXCEPTIONALISM: MAYBE NOT SO MUCH

What Wolf's study does show is that the United States may not be as exceptional as Murray claims. While Wolf shows that developed countries sometimes differ from one another, the United States doesn't stand out as consistently different from other developed countries. The picture of the new upper-middle class given by Murray is pretty consistent with what Wolf gives of the upper-middle class in other developed countries.

WELFARE POLICIES AND ILLEGITIMACY RATES

Wolf's study does justify the inference made by Murray that government welfare policies may make illegitimacy more rational for poor, young women. Again, this is just an inference. Murray doesn't give any evidence of why poor young women in the United States become single mothers. He doesn't interview any single mothers or cite any studies that do. It should be noted that when Max Weber made his distinction between instrumental and value rationality, he argued that the kinds of inferences made by Murray and Wolf were justified only as hypotheses. Demonstrating that certain forms of behavior are consistent with either instrumental or value rationality can be the start of studying why people do what they do. It's the basis of hypotheses as to the motives underlying their actions. To prove such hypotheses, you need to question the people you are studying. Wolf does that in the case of well-educated, upper-class professional women. She interviews such women and asks them why they waited to marry and have children; why they needed nannies or childcare; why they felt they needed to start planning their children's lives from preschool through college. The picture she paints of other women would have been more compelling had she interviewed some of them as well.

STUDY QUESTIONS

1. Why does Wolf think "women" may no longer be a useful theoretical concept?
2. What connections does Wolf try to establish between the professional life of well-educated, upper-middle-class professional women and other aspects of their lives?
3. What does Wolf mean by the concepts of social capital and erotic capital? How does she use these terms in her study?
4. What is meant by modernization theory? How does Wolf use it in *The XX Factor*?
5. What are the major criticisms of modernization theory?
6. Why can't time-use diaries document the reasoning and motivation of social actors?
7. How might Max Weber criticize Wolf's use of the concepts of value rationality and instrumental rationality?

ASSIGNMENTS

1. What is the basic unit of analysis in the reading(s) you are analyzing—a society, a kind of society, or something else?
2. Show how the authors of your reading(s) use theoretical concepts to establish connections between different aspects of the social lives of the actors in their study.

SUGGESTED FURTHER READINGS

"The Rise of Professional Women: Women Now Outpace Men in Every Type of Postsecondary Degree Conferred." *National Journal*.

Black, Sandra E., and Chinhui Juhn. The Rise of Female Professionals: Are Women Responding to Skill Demand?

Gersbuny, Jonathan, and Oriel Sullivan. 1998. "The Sociological Uses of Time-Use Diary Analysis." *European Sociological Review* 14 (1): 69–85.

Weber, Max. 1978. *Economy and Society*, edited by Guenther Roth and Claus Wittich, 26–28 (The Concept of Social Relationship). Berkeley: University of California Press.

IMAGE CREDITS

CHAPTER 11

SHARED PARADIGMS AND OPPOSING PERSPECTIVES

Our curiosities, concerns, and passions play a key role in the selection of which topics we choose to investigate. We employ our sociological imagination to transform these topics into social or intellectual problems. We address these problems by constructing pictures of social life. In our repertoire of theoretical concepts, data are the tools and materials we use to paint these pictures. The methods of inquiry we have mastered determine the options available to us to paint our picture. We use our sociological imagination to select from these materials and tools to choose our approach to constructing a pattern of connections, which constitutes our pictures of social reality. We then argue that the problem we are addressing exists because the social world looks and works the way it is depicted in our picture. For the problem to be solved, we suggest, the social world we have depicted in our picture would have to be altered in the particular ways we specify.

Our examination of Murray's *Coming Apart*, Alexander's *The New Jim Crow* and Wolf's *The XX Factor* demonstrates how varied these pictures can be. It's hard to believe, for instance, that Murray and Alexander are both picturing the social life of the same country. Even more surprisingly, they use similar tools and materials to do so. That is one of the characteristics of much (though certainly not all) contemporary social science. Analysts use the same tools and materials to construct very different pictures of the same social reality. There is often fierce and acrimonious debate and argument over the comparative worth of these pictures. However, such debate and disagreement is only possible because analysts construct their pictures with the same tools and materials. Put differently, underlying the variety of pictures is what T. S. Kuhn called a shared paradigm.

PARADIGMS: T. S. KUHN AND THE HISTORY OF SCIENCE

T. S. Kuhn's (1962) book, *The Structure of Scientific Revolutions*, has probably had as much influence on the social sciences as any book written in the last half century. Yet it isn't about social science. It is a study of the emergence and historical development of the natural sciences. Kuhn argued that the establishment of sciences like physics and chemistry was preceded by long periods in which competing but largely incommensurate ways of seeing the physical or chemical world coexisted. This period was filled with debates about first principles that never seemed to be resolved, because the different views could not really be compared to one another. The adherents of each view largely talked past one another. Sciences were established, Kuhn argued, when a particular work, experiment, or scientific instrument came to be recognized as transcending these debates on first principles, by establishing through example a new way of making sense of a scientific field. Newton's *Principia Mathematica*, Lavoisier's *Chemistry*—these works "served for a time implicitly to define the legitimate problems and methods of a research field for succeeding generations of practitioners" (Kuhn 1962, 10). Such works, Kuhn argued, have two important characteristics. They are able to attract an enduring group of adherents away from competing modes of scientific inquiry, and they are sufficiently open ended to allow for all sorts of problems for these adherents to solve. Kuhn called achievements that shared these characteristics paradigms (10).

Kuhn and the Social Sciences

Kuhn's work spurred a lot of soul searching amongst social scientists. That soul searching was intensified by Kuhn's (1989, 15) comment that "it remains an open question what parts of social science have yet acquired such paradigms at all." Were the social sciences stuck in a preparadigmatic period in which the first principles of the study of social life were endlessly debated but never resolved? Was the study of human social life different in principle from the study of other aspects of the natural world, so that nothing like a social science, at least one modeled on the natural sciences, was possible? Might it be the case that the social sciences would never get beyond these debates on first principles (Kuhn 1989, 216–23)?

We Are What We Study

It seems to me that the study of social life can be said to be different from the study of other natural phenomena in at least two important ways. First, when we study social life, we are what we are studying. It is true that physicists are themselves made up of particles, and chemists combinations of chemical elements. But the particles that physicists study don't debate and argue amongst themselves about how they should behave. Chemical elements don't decide to behave differently. The human beings that social analysts study debate, argue, and make decisions. These debates, arguments, and decisions are an important part of what social scientists study.

The people within Charles Murray's new upper and lower classes have their own ways of making sense of the social world in which they live, as do the highly educated, upper-middle-class professional women Wolf studies. As Alexander tells us, it was African Americans who had been incarcerated and labeled as felons who first introduced her to the idea that drug laws were the new Jim Crow. A large part of what social scientists like Murray, Alexander, and Wolf do is try to make sense of the sense the people they are studying make of their world.

The nature of human social life complicates the task of identifying the paradigmatic elements of social inquiry. Social scientists often use the same categories and concepts that the people they study employ. When they invent their own concepts and categories to make sense of the people they study, the people they study in turn often employ the categories and concepts of the social scientists to make sense of their own world.

PARADIGMS IN THE SOCIAL SCIENCES

Despite these differences in the nature of what natural scientists and social analysts do, many contemporary social scientists may share a common paradigm in Kuhn's sense, or at least there may be a consensus amongst many social scientists on how to view the social world and how to analyze it. Whether or not that is a good thing is an issue we will raise at the end of this chapter and in the chapter that follows it.

A SOCIAL SCIENTIFIC PARADIGM

Kuhn (1962, 4–5) argued that effective research in the natural sciences could scarcely begin until there was widespread consensus amongst the practitioners of a science on the answers to the following questions:

- What are the fundamental entities of which the universe is composed?
- How do these entities interact with each other?
- What questions may legitimately be asked about such entities?
- What techniques may be employed in seeking solutions?

If Kuhn's questions are reformulated somewhat, the studies by Murray, Alexander, and Wolf that we have examined can be said to share the same paradigm, in the sense that they implicitly assume similar answers to the above questions. They view the human social world through the same set of concepts and categories; connect those categories in similar ways; ask similar kinds of questions; and rely on similar kinds of techniques to attempt to formulate answers to the questions they raise. If analysts as different as Murray, Alexander, and Wolf conceive of the social world in the same way, that may indicate that there is something like a shared or at least a dominant paradigm in the social sciences. This is not to say that all social scientists agree in the accounts they give of the social world. As we've seen, social scientific accounts can differ considerably from one another. It is rather to say that these accounts are different solutions to the same kinds of problems. They are able to differ precisely because they look at the social world in similar ways. It is because they share a common way of thinking, speaking and writing about the social world that they are able to understand each other enough to disagree.

FUNDAMENTAL ENTITIES THAT MAKE UP THE SOCIAL UNIVERSE

The universe that social scientists study (and live in) is not made up of stars and planets. The human social world is the universe social scientists study. When social scientists think, speak, and write about this world, they employ theoretical concepts they have created. These concepts aren't images or even descriptions of the social world; they are mechanisms social scientists use to make sense of that world and tools they employ to design pictures of it.

Here I will try to show that Murray, Wolf, Alexander, and many other social scientists use the same set of concepts to construct their pictures of the social world. I've put these concepts in bold to emphasize this point.

SHARED CONCEPTS

Social scientists operating within the dominant paradigm see the social world as made up of **societies**, which can be grouped into different kinds: **developed, developing,** and **underdeveloped.** These **societies** are composed of **social institutions** like families, schools, and businesses. People occupy different **statuses** within these **institutions** and perform different **roles.**

The social universe has temporal and spatial dimensions. Societies have **histories,** as do the people who live in them. Both change over time. People are born, age, and die. Social scientists categorize this **life cycle** in terms of stages: **childhood, adolescence, adulthood,** and **middle and old age.** People who occupy the same span of time are conceived of as **cohorts**. **Societies** and the people in them occupy particular **geographical locales**.

Societies sometimes have a common **culture** and shared **values** and **norms**, though it is possible for that common **culture** to come apart and the shared **value-norm** system to unravel. The **population** of a **society** can be divided hierarchically into groups on the basis of **ethnicity, race, class, caste, gender, elites**, and **masses**.

Though they can be **socialized**, people aren't robots who can be programmed to behave unerringly in particular ways. Humans are **rational actors**. The nature of that **rationality** takes different forms. It can be **instrumentally rational**, the outcome of a calculation of different behaviors' costs and benefits. It can be **value rational**, in accordance with deeply held beliefs, or moral standards. **Social action** takes different forms. Speech and writing are forms of action. So are **work, sex, giving birth, having and raising children**, enjoying **leisure**, and committing **crimes**. **Social actors** accumulate, invest, and spend different **forms of capital**—economic (wealth and income), social (friends and friendship networks), cultural (acquired tastes and preferences), and even erotic (attractiveness). They are themselves often viewed by social scientists (and human resource departments) as **human capital**.

SHARED WAYS OF CONNECTING CONCEPTS

Not only do Murray, Alexander, Wolf, and many other social scientists view the human social world through the same set of concepts, they also agree on the ways these concepts can be related to one another. Theoretical concepts can be combined with one another (**race** or **gender** with **caste**, for instance), related in terms of **equality** and **inequality** (more or less) or **part to whole**, in which the one can be conceived of as a **percentage** of the other. Societies can be conceived of in terms of the **consensus, conflict**, and **separation** of its members. The members of a society can be **rank ordered** (placed higher or lower).

SHARED SET OF PROBLEMS ADDRESSED

The topics social scientists study are those that are thrown up by social life (in a much more direct way, it should be added, than they are in the natural sciences). Social scientists must creatively and imaginatively employ the concepts and data at their disposal and the methods they have mastered to transform those topics into problems. The paradigm within which analysts work does not enable them to address or solve any possible problem. When the soul leaves the body; whether the next toss of a coin will turn up heads or tails; what insights fasting will produce; how our dreams will affect our future are not problems the paradigm we are describing is capable of formulating or solving. It's not that human beings can't conceive of such problems— I just did. It is rather that the paradigm within which most social scientists think makes such formulations seem bizarre, almost absurd.

There is a large number of problems that can be formulated and addressed within this paradigm. A number of problems can be conceived of in terms of the tension between the shared **culture** and the **rank** ordering of the **population** of a **society**. Other problems can be conceived of in terms of the **conflicting** demands made on **governments** increase the national coherence of a **population**; **control** and **maintain** or **alter** and **transform** the system of **rank ordering**; employ political **power** in the **conflict** between **nation states**. Still other problems can be conceived of as emerging out of the tension resulting from the coexistence of a **globalized economy** and multiple **nation states**.

Coming Apart

The problem Charles Murray addresses in *Coming Apart* emerges out of the tension between a shared **culture** and the **rank ordering** of a **population**. He draws two pictures to demonstrate the nature of this problem. The first picture depicts a shared civic **culture** constructed out of a pattern of connections between **values** and **norms**, **statuses** and **roles**, shared tastes and preferences.

The American population was **rank ordered** by **class** in 1963, but the difference in **wealth** and **income** wasn't that great, and people in different **classes** shared the same **beliefs**, **values**, and **norms**; a shared civic **culture** overcame **class** differences. Murray draws a second picture in which civic **culture** is overcome by **class** differences. In this picture, the upper **class** is connected by high levels of **wealth** and **income**; high levels of **educational** attainment; **geographical location**; shared **values**, **norms**, **statuses**, and **roles**; **crime** rates; and tastes and preferences constituting a sub **culture**. They are distinguished from a lower **class** connected by **wealth** and **income**; **educational attainment**; **geographical location**; values, norms, statuses, and **roles**; **and** tastes and preferences constituting a **subculture** very different from that of the upper **class**. The existence of these two separate, **class**-based **subculture** is why the United States is coming apart.

The New Jim Crow

The problem Michelle Alexander addresses in *The New Jim Crow* emerges out of the **conflict** between different **rank-ordered** groups in society who struggle to either maintain or **transform** that **rank ordering**. The picture Alexander constructs to depict her problem takes the form of a **historical** narrative. The common element in this narrative is constructed out of the combination of **caste** and **race**. This **racialized caste** takes different forms in different **historical** periods, but always acts as a form of **social control** of African Americans. At different **historical** times, different **rank-ordered** groups **conflict** with other **rank-ordered groups** to maintain, **transform,** or abolish this **racialized caste**. Alexander explains the problem of high **crime** and **incarceration rates** among **poor, young** African American **males** as the latest form of **racialized caste**. For this problem to be solved, poor blacks and whites need to form a **mass coalition** against **rich** white **elites powerful** enough to eliminate **racialized caste** and create more **equality** amongst the **rank-ordered** groups in US **society**.

The XX Factor

The problem Alison Wolf addresses in *The XX Factor* emerges out of the growing **inequality** between **classes** in **developed societies**, resulting in part from the changing position of some **women** in those societies. To address this problem, Wolf draws a picture of the lives led by **women** through most of human **history**. She pictures **women's** lives as defined by their membership in a **gendered caste** through which the **status** and **roles** they could occupy were determined by their **gender**. Wolf then pictures a **cohort** of women in **developed societies** (her hinge generation) who became **adults** in the 1970s and managed to escape the confines of this **gendered caste** and alter the **statuses** and **roles** they could occupy. They did this by achieving high levels of **educational attainment**, a large share of the **jobs** opened up by the global **economy,** and high levels of **wealth** and **income** in the process.

Wolf connects the **occupational status** of this new group of women to changes in the **age** at which they **marry**, their **sex** lives, their **child-rearing** practices, and the way they spend their **leisure** time. These connections **separate** them from other women who continued to occupy **statuses** and **roles** defined by their **gender**, while more closely **connecting** them to the men who share their **class** position. Thus, Wolf presents a picture of **developed societies** in which the rise of a particular group of **well-educated, well-paid professional women** had the unintended consequence of widening the **separation** between social **classes**.

Data Created and Collected

Data is not social reality, though the intent behind collecting data is to be as descriptive as possible about the aspects of social reality that the people collecting the data and the people employing these collections think important. In the modern world, governments keep extensive records on their citizens. In addition to government records, major universities have research centers that collect data on particular topics. Independent research institutes, some with an avowed ideological bent, some without, also construct collections of data on particular topics. International organizations like the United Nations and the Organisation for Economic Co-operation and Development (OECD) construct their own data sets. Social scientists make extensive use of these records as data that they employ to answer their questions. Corporations possess extensive data collections on people, but much of this data is proprietary and difficult to access.

Techniques and Methods Used to Address Problems

Murray, Alexander, Wolf, and many other social scientists employ similar techniques and methods to address social and intellectual problems. These techniques are usually divided into qualitative and quantitative types. Among the qualitative research techniques employed are structured and unstructured interviews, focus groups, self-study, and ethnographic methods like participant observation, in which the analyst spends long periods of time with the people he or she is studying, sometimes with the aid of an informant (one of the people the researcher is studying). The researcher takes detailed notes on the observations he or she makes and reports on the findings based on these notes.

Quantitative methods are designed to be an analog of the experimental method employed in the natural sciences. The use of quantitative methods involves the operationalization of theoretical concepts in ways that allow the collection of data that can be measured or counted. This allows the social analyst to use mathematical, particularly statistical, operations and computer software to solve the problems they address. Quantitative methodology involves the use of sampling techniques and the construction of surveys based on carefully designed questionnaires, the answers to which can be coded. A key objective of quantitative methodology is the production of results that have high reliability and can be replicated (USC Libraries Research Guide, http://libguides.usc.edu/sociology).

Most analysts employ a mix of qualitative and quantitative techniques, and they all wrestle with the same kinds of problems when they employ these techniques. In-depth interviews and participant observation provide detailed information on a limited number of subjects. The problem is that it is not always clear how much the information gathered using such techniques can be generalized. Quantitative data, by contrast, even if it is based on sampling (which it often is) is easier to generalize to larger populations. However, these generalizations are based on questions and constructs developed by data collectors, rather than the views of the people being studied. My point is that most social scientists (though again, certainly not all) employ the same kinds of techniques to answer the same kinds of questions; face the same kinds of difficulties trying to do so; and try to resolve those problems in the same kinds of ways.

THINKING OUTSIDE THE PARADIGMATIC BOX

Murray and Alexander, to some extent, think outside this paradigmatic box in limited but important ways. Murray uses the concept of innate intelligence, which is not part of the repertoire of most social scientists. In principle, most social scientists grant that humans have innate capacities, but they rarely see the social world in terms of these capacities. Murray may be right that in the future advances in the cognitive sciences and sociobiology may change the way social scientists view the social world. However, if they do, the paradigm through which many contemporary social scientists currently view the world will be fundamentally transformed. Kuhn called such transformations scientific revolutions.

The mix of techniques and the form in which Michelle Alexander presents her argument is somewhat different than those employed by most contemporary social scientists. This is probably because Alexander trained in law, a field which, while closely related to social science, remains outside of it. Alexander's study takes the form of something closer to a legal brief than a social scientific study. She uses some of the concepts, data, and techniques common to social scientists (a combination of in-depth, unstructured interviews, secondary sources, and US government databases) to construct her brief. However, she uses a number of court decisions and opinions as well. There is nothing wrong with this; it is just not part of most social scientists' repertoire. It isn't surprising that the same set of concepts, connections between concepts, data sources, and techniques can be employed to paint very different pictures of social life. For a shared paradigm to work, it must be open-ended enough to allow for different solutions to similar problems.

Pros and Cons of the Dominant Paradigm

Establishing that a shared paradigm underlies even a large number of social scientific studies does not in itself prove the value of that paradigm. To say that a paradigm is a particular way of making sense of social life is not to say that it is the only or best way to make sense of social life. We should at least hold open the possibility that different theoretical concepts, different connections between concepts, different questions asked about social life, and different techniques for arriving at solutions to different problems might give us different and perhaps more insightful views of human social life.

To say that most contemporary social scientists use the same paradigm to make sense of the social world does not mean that the paradigm they share is the best one to use to make such sense. In *The Structure of Scientific Revolutions* T. S. Kuhn said that doing scientific work within an established paradigm is akin to solving a puzzle (35–42). It is easy to see the parallels. Using a set of theoretical concepts, connections, and techniques to address a set number of problems is very much like trying to solve very complex puzzles. However, if the pieces of the puzzle don't fit, it may be time to abandon or radically alter the puzzle itself. We need to keep in mind why we work so hard to try to solve such puzzles. It isn't, or in my view, shouldn't be, just for the fun or challenge of it. Our objective should be to use our curiosities, concerns, passions, and sociological imaginations to make sense of social life, to understand and help solve social and intellectual problems and to advance social justice. When, despite our best efforts (and those of many other social analysts), we and they can't make the pieces of the puzzle fit together, the fault may lie in the puzzle (the paradigm). It may be that major changes in social life have thrown up new problems unsolvable within the existing paradigm. Solving the problem may require changing the paradigm.

Study Questions

1. What is a paradigm and what, according to Kuhn, are its defining characteristics?
2. What are the essential differences between the social sciences and the natural sciences?
3. How and in what sense can Charles Murray, Michelle Alexander, and Alison Wolf be said to be operating within the same paradigm?
4. What kinds of questions can be answered working within this paradigm, and what kinds can't?

ASSIGNMENTS

1. Does the author of the reading(s) you have selected work within the same paradigm as do Murray, Alexander, and Wolf?
2. Can the problems you want to address in your research proposal be addressed within the above paradigm? If so, how so? If not, why not?

SUGGESTED FURTHER READINGS

Kuhn, T. S. 1962. *The Structure of Scientific Revolutions*, 1–10 (A Role for History). Chicago: University of Chicago Press.

Kuhn, T. S. 1989. *The Road Since Structure*, edited by James Conant and John Haugeland, 216–24 (The Natural and The Human Sciences). Chicago: University of Chicago Press.

University of Southern California Libraries Research Guide: http://libguides.usc.edu/writingguide/quantitative

Winch, Peter. 1958. *The Idea of a Social Science*, 40–66 (The Nature of Meaningful Behavior). London: Routledge.

CHAPTER 12

MARGARET KOVACH'S *INDIGENOUS METHODOLOGIES: CHARACTERISTICS, CONVERSATIONS, AND CONTEXTS*

THINKING OUTSIDE THE PARADIGMATIC BOX: ARE THERE DIFFERENT WAYS OF KNOWING?

I have suggested that Murray's *Coming Apart*, Alexander's *The New Jim Crow* and Wolf's *The XX Factor*, for all their differences, share a common paradigm. Many other works of contemporary social science could be said to share this same paradigm. This paradigm is composed of theoretical concepts designed to help make sense of contemporary developed societies. Indeed, the concept of "developed society" is itself one of those concepts. However, the further removed such a paradigm is from the kind of society it was designed to understand, the less useful it becomes. That is no doubt what Jürgen Habermas (1996, 40) meant when he made the following argument: "when a theoretical framework constructed of historically substantive concepts is to be used for the analysis of historically distant and culturally alien contexts; in the altered context, the tool becomes particularly blunt."

Indigenous communities would constitute, in Habermas' terms, "a culturally alien context." It's not that the paradigm I described in the last chapter can't be used to make sense of Indigenous communities. The discipline of cultural anthropology was developed with just such an objective in mind. However, some scholars from these communities, including Margaret Kovach, complain that such traditional ethnographies were studies of the "other" (Kovach 2009, 27). The studies of the founders of cultural anthropology, they argue, were attempts by Westerners to understand other peoples in Western terms.

A number of contemporary Indigenous scholars want to understand the communities from which they have come on their own terms. These Indigenous scholars recognize that they themselves exist in two different worlds. Trained in Western universities, they claim an identity with the communities of their origin. They are part of what Margaret Kovach refers to as an urban Indigenous population (38). Kovach is herself an urban Indigenous scholar. Her birth parents were Plains Cree, and she wants to understand both herself and the Indigenous community with which she

Figure 12.1: Totem Pole

identifies in its own terms. She and a number of other urban Indigenous scholars with similar objectives have come to the following conclusions, which they want to convey to the rest of us: You can't understand people like us in the same way you understand yourselves. We can't understand ourselves and the communities from which we came in the ways the people who conquered and marginalized us understand the social world. We can best understand ourselves and our communities in our own terms.

ARE THERE DIFFERENT WAYS OF KNOWING?

Is this possible? Karl Popper (1957), one of the most influential philosophers of the last century, dismissed such an idea as historicism. He argued that all humans think in the same way. Put yourself in the position of Julius Caesar with his goals and objectives and you would act and think in the same way he did, Popper (1976, 103) argued.

Scholars like Kovach, contrary to Popper, argue that there are different ways of knowing and that people in Indigenous communities think and experience the world on different terms than do Westerners. In *Indigenous Methodologies*, Kovach tries to explain this different way of thinking and how to use it to understand Indigenous communities on their own terms. Furthermore, she argues that it is possible to translate one way of knowing into another. Kovach addresses the problem of presenting Indigenous knowledge and ways of knowing in a manner translatable into Western terms (Kovach 2009, 40). She tries to make room for both while bridging the epistemic differences between them (29).

TWO DIFFERENT WAYS OF KNOWING

Kovach readily acknowledges "the complexities of researching across knowledge paradigms" (31). Even on first approximation, Indigenous knowledge, the form it takes, and the methods through which it is acquired, seems radically different from those with which we are familiar. In the contemporary West, we separate the sacred and the profane. We strive for universal forms of knowledge that transcend space and time.

While there are contemporary Western scholars who argue that such universals are unattainable when studying the human social world, these scholars base their argument on a differentiation of the human social realm from that of other aspects of nature for which such universals can in principle be found. We separate the knower from what can be known, the subjective from the objective. Our criteria for knowledge is truth supported by objective evidence, preferably conveyed in the form of syllogisms or mathematical formulas.

Indigenous knowledge is very different. Not only is it holistic, their wholes are very different from those with which we are familiar. The Indigenous whole is a synthesis of the material and the spiritual, the cognitive and experiential, the internal and the external. Indigenous knowledge is subjective by its very nature. It is never universal but is always limited to particular places and communities. The Indigenous self is always a self-in-relation to a particular place and people.

Indigenous knowledge comes through many portals—dreams, fasting, water walks, sweat lodges. It is conveyed in the form of stories told and retold by members of the same tribe, those living and their ancestors.

Given these wide differences, it is hard not to share Kovach's wonder at how difficult it must have been for Indigenous peoples and their European conquerors to understand each other (25).

Navigating Two Different Worlds

Kovach and Indigenous scholars like her face the personal conflict of navigating two different worlds—the communities from which they come and academia. These different worlds have different expectations for research. In academia, the expectation is that research will be published in books and journals. In indigenous communities, knowledge is transmitted in oral form. In academia, research findings are often abstracted from their context. Indigenous knowledge is defined by its context. Indigenous knowledge is web-like rather than lineal in its structure (47).

Despite the difficulties, Kovach finds the effort to understand Indigenous thinking on its own terms worthwhile, not only for people like her, but for non-indigenous people as well. "Indigenous methodologies prompt Western traditions to engage in reflexive self-study, to consider a research paradigm outside the Western tradition that offers a systematic approach to understanding the world" (29).

The Decolonizing Lens

In approaching Indigenous knowledge, Kovach tries to take the advice she once gave to one of her students: "Start where you are, it will take you where you need to go" (10). She gives the example of her colleague, Michael Hart, who said to her, "I am Indigenous. I speak English. That is where I come from" (69). Another colleague, Graham Smith, also starts with first principles: "I am arguing for my language, knowledge and culture and against reproducing colonizing forces in my research" (90).

To get from where they start to where they want to go, Kovach thinks that Indigenous scholars need a "decolonizing lens." They need this not only because colonial relationships are reproduced inside the universities in which they study, but also because they are reproduced inside the Indigenous researchers themselves (29). Kovach thinks some aspects of Western qualitative research are congruent enough with Indigenous ways of knowing to provide a bridge from one to the other (25–27). She identifies aspects of phenomenology, feminist theory, critical theory, and Marxism as potentially providing such a bridge. It is not these theories as wholes that Kovach thinks can perform this function. It is particular aspects of each that she thinks useful. She likes phenomenology's emphasis on the necessity of capturing "the self as it comes to know" (18) and its emphasis on the importance of the consciousness of intention to the research process (42). What she likes about feminist theory is that it "allows feminist researchers to share the experience of conducting research and their own subjective experience with their research participants" (33). She thinks that critical theory, when used as a decolonizing lens, encourages a critical self-consciousness in the researcher. It has the potential to keep Indigenous scholars constantly aware of the political nature of their work (85).

In addition to helping the Indigenous researcher bring to consciousness those elements of a colonial way of thinking which have become part of their perspective on social reality, Kovach thinks a decolonizing lens has other benefits. It has the potential to bring Indigenous knowledge out of the margins and to create a space for it within the university (82, 85). It can help satisfy the demand of Indigenous communities for a decolonizing outcome to the research of Indigenous scholars (86). This can be accomplished in a number of ways. Indigenous scholars can document the historical experience of colonial relations. They can employ the Marxist concept of ideological hegemony to demonstrate how teaching and learning in Indigenous communities have been used to maintain and reproduce Western ways of thinking, and to suppress Indigenous ways of thinking within the school system (89, 91).

While important, a decolonizing lens is merely a mechanism for getting at Kovach's real objective: Indigenous knowledge and ways of knowing. Such knowledge is tribal-centered rather than centered on the relationship between tribes and their colonizers (80).

INDIGENOUS WAYS OF KNOWING

Indigenous ways of knowing cannot be completely standardized because they exist in different tribal forms, each rooted in particular communities and places. That said, tribal forms of knowledge share a common enough framework and outlook to sharply differentiate them from Western approaches to knowledge, like those exemplified by Murray, Alexander, and Wolf.

KNOWLEDGE AS A WAY OF BEING

Cognition is just a part of the Indigenous way of learning and knowing. Indigenous knowledge makes no distinction between inward and outward knowing (Kovach 2009, 67). Much of Indigenous knowing is internal, personal, and experiential (43). It is about living life each day according to certain values (62). Knowing is a process of being (67). For Indigenous peoples, knowledge is that which helps them move forward with their lives (72). In Indigenous communities, thinking well, living well, and being a good person are aspects of the same. "The ideal Native American personality is one who is kind, who puts the group first, who is friendly, who is

Decolonizing Lens

Phenomenology: The Self as it comes to know; consciousness of intention

Feminist Theory: Researcher and research participants share the research experience

Critical Theory: Encourages critical self-awareness in the researcher

Marxism: Concept of Ideological hegemony

Figure 12.2: Decolonizing Lens

'steeped in spiritual and ritual knowledge' who is easy going and has a good sense of humor" (62–63).

UNDERSTANDING THE WORLD WITHOUT HARMING IT

While Indigenous knowledge is personal and experiential, it is a process of 'self-in-relation' as well (14). It is nested and created within the context of relationships with other living beings (47). Part of knowing is living according to the underlying values of your community and maintaining good relations with it (63). A key objective of Indigenous knowing is "seeking ways to understand the world without harming it" (11).

Indigenous knowing comes out of the proper relationship between a people, their way of using language, and their land (17). Indigenous people do not separate reason and spirit (77). Indigenous people conceive of place as alive and imbued with spirit. Place is connected to everything that occupies it. Place informs. It provides a line through time connecting a people to their ancestors (61–62).

SPIRIT AND PLACE

Each nation has its "iskonikanik," which connects a specific place, language, and set of relationships (73). When you introduce yourself in Nehiyawewin, for instance, you state your name and your community of belonging, your iskonikanik: "the little piece of land that the white settlers didn't want" (73).

Because Indigenous knowledge makes no rigid distinction between the everyday and the sacred, it is important to connect physical space with sacred space. Indigenous knowledge is something that occurs between the person and the sacred world (72).

Ceremony and Ritual

In Indigenous thought, ceremony and ritual are mechanisms for connecting people to the spiritual world. Pipes, songs, rattles, and plant and animal medicines are tools that act as catalysts to connect the person to the sacred world. They are physical manifestations of sacred experiences. The passing of these tools from person to person establishes a spiritual connection between people and spiritual space. In Indigenous thought, there is no separation between the social, the material, and the spiritual world. In Indigenous thought, the world and everything in it is alive.

The Telling of Stories

Indigenous knowledge is contained in and communicated through the telling of stories. Stories are a legitimate form of understanding. While Indigenous stories don't have conventional boundaries, there are many different kinds of them. There are stories of creation, teaching stories, personal narratives, and stories about places. These stories are told and retold over generations, connecting people with each other and with their ancestors (Kovach 2009, 94). Indigenous stories don't take the form of linear narrative. They are more about place and people than time.

To come to know an Indigenous community in its own terms, one must elicit and make sense of its stories. Before one can begin to do that, investigators must prepare themselves. They must reflect on the purpose of their investigations both for themselves and for the community they are investigating. Research must fill a gap; it must serve a need of the community being studied.

The Elders as Gatekeepers of Knowledge

To elicit stories from community members, permission must be granted by the community elders. There are protocols that must be obeyed. For the Cree, tobacco must be exchanged and smoked. This signifies respect and is a way of establishing trust.

The investigator must begin by telling their own story to the elders and connecting their story to the purpose of their study. This will be followed by a conversation between the investigators and the elders about how the study will benefit the community.

If permission is granted, the investigator, in consultation with the elders, will select participants with whom they will share a talking circle. Once gifts are given, the investigator begins by telling their story to the members of the talking circle and connecting it to the topic and purpose of the study. The participants are then given the opportunity to tell their stories in their own way and to relate their stories to the topic and the purpose of the study as they see fit. In this way power is shared between the researchers and the participants (125).

TALKING CIRCLES

Approaching topics through talking circles can be a lengthy and laborious process. From the Western perspective, talking circles can appear unnecessarily time consuming and inefficient. Jeannine Carriere's experience as a child welfare specialist attending a Prairie Child Welfare symposium illustrates this point. For the first two days of the conference, the aboriginal people attending sat quietly but restlessly listening to government representatives and university specialists lecture on child welfare. It soon became clear to Carriere that the conference was going nowhere. The Indigenous people were completely turned off by the process.

On the final day of the conference, at Jeannine Carriere's urging, the conference format was changed. "We sat in a circle on the last day, and I can't even remember how many people there were but it was the largest circle I ever sat in ... everybody started talking about their own experiences as opposed to the policy and what should be done in practice. It was more like 'This is my experience with child welfare.' I felt this thing rising in me because I thought, 'Can I really do this? Can I really talk about my family experience of being adopted and reconnecting and the whole experience around that?' As the circle kept going, it got closer to my turn, and I knew I didn't have a choice. I had to be authentic in what I said, and it had to be about my experience" (Kovach, 104).

I can imagine a possible reaction of the government representatives and university specialists to Carriere's participation in the conference. I could certainly see their being frustrated. They might well have thought that she led the conference off topic. On the last day, at her urging, the conference got away from a discussion of policy and degenerated into an endless telling of personal stories that went nowhere. To top it all off, Carriere told her own personal story and in doing so acted completely unprofessionally.

I don't know that this was the reaction of the government representatives and university professionals, but it would be a perfectly understandable way to react—understandable, that is, from a conventional Western bureaucratic and academic perspective. The point is that Indigenous people have a very different perspective. From their perspective, stories about their personal experiences with the child welfare system were not off topic. Such stories should have been the topic. Telling personal stories is the Indigenous way of addressing any topic.

Using Indigenous methods to study Indigenous communities takes the form of conversations and exchanging stories. Since these conversations will eventually be written down (a concession to Western ways) the participants must be shown the transcript of the conversations and be allowed to make corrections to it. Since the conversations will inevitably have to be condensed, the condensed version of the conversations must be shown to and approved by the participants as well.

EVALUATING THE VALIDITY OF KNOWLEDGE

The validity of these stories is judged differently in the Indigenous community than it would be in conventional academia. In the Indigenous community, truth is established not by objective proof, but through sacred commitments between the storyteller and those who listen to their stories. Truth is not abstracted from life. By abiding by the tribal protocols, the teller makes a solemn commitment that the story they tell is true as far as they know it.

The acquisition of knowledge comes through reflection on these stories. What is their meaning? What do they say about the community? There is sacredness to Indigenous research, a binding of ceremony, spirit, land, place, nature, relationships, language, dreams, and stories.

After a conversation with her colleague, Laara Fitznor, it occurred to Kovach that "meaning making in Indigenous inquiry involved observation, sensory experience, contextual knowledge, and recognition of patterns. It drew upon external and internal sources, was highly interpretive and combined with a form of inductive analysis" (Kovach 2009, 140).

INDIGENOUS KNOWLEDGE AND WESTERN ACADEMIA: TENSIONS,

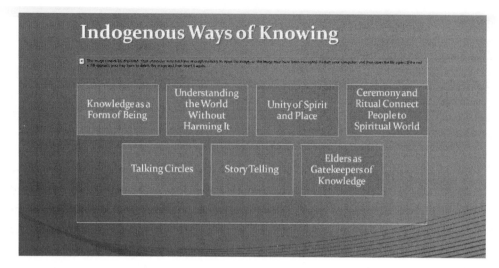

Figure 12.3: Indigenous Knowledge

CONFLICTS, AND COMPROMISES

Indigenous researchers grapple with how to present research in a way that honors tribal knowledge yet is understandable for non-Indigenous people, including those in the universities where they study (Kovach 2009, 140). Achieving both these goals inevitably involves compromises.

The stories in which Indigenous knowledge is contained are meant to be told orally. "In the oral tradition, stories can never be decontextualized from the teller. They are the active agents within a relational world. ... Oral stories are born of connections within the world, and are thus recounted relationally. They tie us with our past and provide a basis for continuity with future generations" (94).

But times change, and if these Indigenous stories are to be heard they need to be written down (102). Transferring what was meant to be told orally to written text is a complex process. It is easy to lose what is essential to the oral tradition in the process. "It is often the case in mainstream scholarship, that once a story is shared and recorded, 'facts' are extracted and the remaining 'superfluous' data set aside. ... The bundle is plundered, the voice silenced, bits are extracted to meet empirical needs, and the story dies" (101).

To capture the insider's perspective contained in Indigenous stories, the written account must adhere as closely as possible to the spoken story. The reader should be told that the style of the story is "casual, familiar and marked by numerous interruptions and exchange" (100). Capturing in writing the nonverbal nuances of stories and conversations is a challenge, "yet this form contains much knowledge" (100).

REPLICATION AND SAMPLING

It is impossible to replicate studies conducted from the Indigenous perspective because the researcher, the participants, and the community are integral parts of the study. The Indigenous form of knowledge is subjective by design. The investigators' self-conscious and critical reflection is essential to any knowledge obtained. As a result, there can be no objectivity in the Western sense.

If the object of a study is the uncovering of an Indigenous way of thinking, conventional sampling techniques probably won't work. Participants for the study need to be selected on the basis of their position in the community. The study will consist of give-and-take conversation and the exchange of stories between researcher and participants. Focus groups, surveys, interviews, and polling probably won't work, either.

PORTALS OF KNOWLEDGE

Crucial to understanding another way of thinking is a willing suspension of disbelief. You have to accept, at least provisionally, the possibility that knowledge may come from many places and try to make sense of that. Is it possible to learn something about someone's subjective state from their dreams? Indigenous people aren't alone in thinking so. Can dreams alter reality? They can if they are interpreted and if attempts are made to conduct future action on the basis of those interpretations. As one of the founders of American sociology, W. I. Thomas, said, "If men define situations as real, they are real in their consequences" (William and Dorothy Thomas, 1929, 572). Can fasting alter our subjective state? I have no doubt of it. Are the insights we have in this changed state more valid than those we have in our "normal" state? That may be hard to say, but it is not hard to conceive of people thinking that they might be. After all, it is certainly possible that long solitary walks in the woods, meditation, and periods of silent contemplation might help stimulate insight.

INDIGENOUS STANDARDS OF ETHICAL INQUIRY

In the West, the ethical mandates of scientific studies involving research participants are designed to protect the participants from being damaged in some way by their participation in the study. Such studies conducted under institutional auspices ordinarily must be sanctioned by institutional review boards. These boards review proposed research to ensure that the participants in studies are not harmed in any way; that their participation is voluntary; that they have given their informed consent to participate in the study; and that they aren't in any way deceived by the investigator conducting the research (Babbie 2010, 64–75).

Mostly, the ethics of studying Indigenous communities on their own terms are additional to those which would generally apply in social scientific inquiry. But the difference in paradigms also results in additional ethical conflicts and tensions.

EXPERIMENTS AND SURVEYS

Experiments and surveys are, in an important sense, done to or on participants. That is why the participants in studies that take these forms require protection from harm, deception, and abuse. When Indigenous communities are studied on their own terms, the ethical strictures must cover the community studied, and the elders of the community need to define those strictures. "Doing no harm" is not enough for the elders of Indigenous communities. The elders in these communities require those who study them and the studies they perform to "do good," and they reserve the right to determine what that good is.

ANONYMITY

Ethics boards in Western institutions usually try to protect either the anonymity or the confidentiality of the participants in studies. This often isn't possible and doesn't make sense when Indigenous communities are studied on their own terms. Indigenous knowledge comes in the form of stories, the veracity of which is guaranteed by the integrity of the teller. Community elders play a role in the selection of participants in such studies. The participants are chosen because of their position in the community. The stories they tell are usually told in story circles. The storytellers pledge that the stories they tell are true as far as they know. Under these conditions, the storytellers cannot be anonymous. Their identities cannot remain confidential.

INVESTIGATORS AND STUDY PARTICIPANTS

In Western institutions, the relationship between investigators and study participants is distant, formal, and neutral. That cannot be the case in Indigenous studies conducted with Indigenous methodologies. The investigators tell their story before the participants tell theirs. They are part of the study. The relationship between the investigator, study participants, community elders, and the community itself is one of shared cooperation, trust, and respect, not formality, distance, and neutrality.

TELL ALL?

In Western academic institutions, there is something like an implicit obligation on the part of investigators "to tell all." An investigator who conceals information learned about a community under study because the leaders of the community think the information might put the community in a bad light faces a serious ethical quandary. By withholding such information, many would argue, they are giving a false impression of what is really going on.

The elders in Indigenous communities view studies done about their communities in very different terms. Indigenous knowledge is sacred. What parts of it can be released to outsiders is determined by them and is explicitly intended to create a favorable view of their community in the outside world. Investigators are trusted to tell outsiders only what the elders agree can be told. Moreover, investigators must agree to tell what can be told in a form that is accessible to community members.

THE INDIGENOUS IMAGINATION

Kovach and other Indigenous scholars, like Western scholars, are motivated by curiosity, concern, and passion. They are curious as to whether or not Indigenous thinking can be understood on its own terms and translated into terms outsiders can understand. They are concerned about the many social problems faced by Indigenous communities. They are passionate in their desire to pursue social justice for these communities by keeping, maintaining, and continuing traditional ways of knowing and living. For that to happen, they think these ways of knowing and living need to be understood and respected by outsiders.

While Western social scientists exercise their sociological imagination to connect their personal problems and situations to the social issues and problems faced by the societies in which they live, Indigenous scholars exercise what I will call an Indigenous imagination. They employ their Indigenous imagination to construct a self-in-relation to their study, to those participating in it, and to the community being studied. They employ an Indigenous imagination to develop a critical self-consciousness of their study, and of themselves. Are they and their studies "doing good?" Are they making the communities they study better, and themselves better, through their studies?

What Is to Be Learned from the Indigenous Way of Thinking and Indigenous Ways of Studying Thinking?

Whether or not it is possible for different groups of people to think differently depends on what one means by thinking differently. Popper might well have said that, if we know the situation and objectives faced by Indigenous thinkers, we can understand what they are thinking in that situation. However, that borders on tautology. It is in effect saying that if we think as Indigenous thinkers think, we think as Indigenous thinkers think. In practical terms, Indigenous ways of thinking seem to me in important ways different from Western ways of thinking. Moreover, the effort to understand Indigenous thinking in its own terms is worthwhile for the reasons Kovach suggests: to consider a research paradigm outside the Western tradition prods us to engage in reflexive self-study of our own ways of thinking.

Reflections on Indigenous Ways of Thinking

So prodded, let me share my reflections. I think the Indigenous linkage between thinking well, living well, and being a good person is worth emulating. It reminds me of the ancient Greeks' attempt to address the questions of how we should live and how we should live together.

The Indigenous emphasis on maintaining a critical awareness of our studies and our relationship to our studies also seems to me worthwhile. Are we making the communities we study better, and ourselves better, through our studies? These questions are worth asking. The objective of "seeking ways to understand the world without harming it" is also a good one to pursue (Kovach 2009, 11).

Study Questions

1. Identify the Indigenous answers to the paradigmatic questions suggested by Kuhn:
   • What are the entities of which the Indigenous universe consists?
   • How are these entities connected?
   • What questions can be asked of these entities?
   • What methods can be employed in answering these questions?
2. What are basic differences between the Indigenous paradigm and the one that Murray, Alexander, and Wolf work within?

Figure 12.4: Inuit People

3. What questions can be answered and problems addressed within the Indigenous paradigm that can't be asked or addressed within the Western paradigm?

ASSIGNMENTS

1. Are there things to be learned from the Indigenous way of knowing? What are they?
2. Do the readings you are examining meet the ethical strictures of Indigenous ways of knowing?
3. How might the study you are proposing incorporate these ethical strictures?

SUGGESTED FURTHER READINGS

Graham, Mary. 2008. "Some Thoughts about the Philosophical Underpinnings of Aboriginal Worldviews." *Australian Humanities Review* 45. http://www.australianhumanitiesreview .org/archive/Issue-November-2008/graham.html.

Haig-Brown, Celia. 2008. "Taking Indigenous Thought Seriously: A Rant on Globalization with Some Cautionary Notes." *Journal of the Association of Curriculum Studies*. Toronto: York University.

Kovach, Margaret. 2009. *Indigenous Methodologies: Characteristics, Conversations, and Contexts*, 55–75 (Epistemology and Research: Centring Tribal Knowledge). Toronto, Canada: University of Toronto Press.

Popper, Karl. 1957. *The Poverty of Historicism*, 4–31 (The Anti-Naturalist Doctrines of Historicism). Boston and New York: Routledge.

Image Credits

CHAPTER 13

THEORIZING: UNCOVERING, DESCRIBING, EVALUATING, AND DOING

I designed this book to provide some suggestions for how to get at the social theorizing present in all social studies, even those directed at a general readership. When you examine articles in academic books and journals directed at a more specialized readership, you may find the arguments more abstract, the vocabulary more technical, and the methodological techniques more sophisticated than those used in the studies I have analyzed here. That said, if you have a firm grasp on what we have covered here, you are off to a good start. To make sure you have that grasp, let's go over the steps I've suggested you follow when you are trying to uncover, describe, and evaluate the social theorizing in a study. Then I'll make some suggestions as to how to do your own theorizing by constructing a research project proposal. Now is the time to collect all your notes on the assignments at the end of each chapter. They should provide you with most of the material you will need in order to uncover, describe, and evaluate the study you have been analyzing, and to write your research project proposal.

UNCOVERING THE THEORIZING UNDERLYING A SOCIAL STUDY

Curiosities, Concerns, and Passions

Remember that the authors of social studies probably began to study social life for many of the same reasons you did. They became self-consciously reflective about their own social lives and those of the people around them. In our terms, they became curious about the social world, how it works; why it works the way it does; whether it works the same way everywhere; whether it has always worked that way; and whether it will continue to work that way in the future. As we sometimes do when we look at our lives, ourselves, and the world around us, they may have become troubled and concerned by what they saw. Aspects of the social world and their own lives didn't seem to be working the way they thought they should, or the way most people said they should. Something appeared to be wrong. They may have become convinced that the way things did work was unfair and unjust. They didn't want to accept things the way they were just because they were that way. They thought things ought to be different, and they wanted to help make them different.

If you can identify the curiosity, concern, and passion that lie behind a study, you have taken the first step to making sense of it. How do you go about making such identifications? The author will often tell you in the preface or introduction to the study. These days, there is a good chance the author has a website or a Facebook page. If all else fails, don't be afraid to Google! In any event, the study itself should reveal the curiosities, concerns, and passions that motivated its author to write it.

Topic

The next step involved in uncovering the theorizing is to identify the topic of the study. Remember Baxandall's (1985) account of how painters and architects begin the construction of their objects. They begin with a charge, which we have compared to a topic. Just as there are lots of different kinds of structures designed to perform lots of different functions from which architects can choose, and different possible kinds of subjects for painters to paint, social life provides plenty of topics worth studying. How do students of social life select from amongst them? Usually and hopefully, they select their topic on the basis of the connection between the topic, their social curiosities, concerns, and passions, and the topic's social import. If you can connect the topic of the study you are analyzing with the curiosities, concerns, and passions of its author, you have taken another step toward uncovering the theorizing that underlies the study.

Transforming a Topic into a Problem

An important part of social theorizing involves the use of sociological imagination to fuse curiosity, concern, and passion with a topic, and thereby transform that topic into a problem. You need to determine how the author of your study transformed its topic into a social or intellectual problem, and describe that problem.

Selecting Concepts, Employing Methods, and Data

Once you have identified and described the problem your study addresses, you need to identify the concepts, methodological approach, and data the author of the study you are analyzing employs to construct the picture or pictures of social life that constitute the solution to the problem addressed. Remember, by methods we mean both the approach taken (comparative, historical, case study, ethnographic study) as well as the methods used to create the data used in the study. If the author of the study you are analyzing created their own data, describe what kinds of data they created, and how they did it. If the study relies largely on data sources collected by others, say so, and say also where the author got this data. Addressing the problem addressed in the study involves the construction of a picture of how a given part of the social world looks and works, which reveals why the problem being addressed exists. What concepts, data, and methods does the author use to construct that picture?

A Pattern of Connections

This picture consists of a pattern of connections between social phenomena that, in the author's view, accounts for the social conditions that have given rise to the problem being addressed. Detecting and describing that pattern of connections and its relationship to the social or intellectual problem being addressed is central to uncovering and describing the social theorizing underlying a social study.

Proposed Solutions

Finally, you need to determine whether or not the author of the study you are examining proposes a solution the problem the study addresses. Optimally, the solution should specify how that part of social reality pictured in the study would have to be changed if the problem is to be solved.

THE EVALUATION OF THE THEORIZING UNDERLYING A SOCIAL STUDY

Being Mindful and Reflective in Your Evaluation

When you are evaluating the theorizing that has gone into a social study, it is important to be mindful and reflective. The author of the study you are evaluating isn't the only one with curiosities, concerns, and passions; you have them, too. The author of the work you are analyzing wrote it from a particular perspective, and you evaluate it from one as well. It is important to be mindful of both perspectives when you do your evaluating. As I said when I made my evaluation of Murray's *Coming Apart* and Alexander's *The New Jim Crow*, I think you should try to make the best possible case for the theorizing done from perspectives different from your own, and be as critical as possible in your evaluation of the pictures constructed from perspectives you share.

Make a Judgment of the Importance of the Problem Addressed in the Study You Analyze. Defend That Judgment.

When evaluating a social study, it is important to make a judgment on the importance of the problem the study addresses. I didn't explicitly make this judgment in the case of the studies authored by Murray, Alexander, Wolf, and Kovach, because I thought the importance of the problems they addressed was self-evident. That isn't always the case. Everyone is free to address any problem they wish, but every analyst is equally free to evaluate the social significance of that problem. However imaginative, skillful, and well informed the theorizing, if the problem at which this imagination, skill, and knowledge is directed is insignificant, then the theorizing is just that: imaginative, skillful, well informed, and insignificant. "As in all other sciences, we are, in the social sciences, either successful or unsuccessful, interesting or dull, fruitful or unfruitful, in exact proportion to the significance or interest of the problems we are concerned with; and also of course, in exact proportion to the honesty, directness and simplicity with which we tackle these problems" (Popper 1976, 89).

The Use of the Sociological Imagination

Once you have made a judgment as to the importance of the problem being addressed, you can begin your evaluation of how well the author of the study you are examining fuses her or his curiosity, concern, and passion with the study's topic to transform it into a social or intellectual problem. Such a transformation involves imagination of a particular type, what C. Wright Mills (1959) called a sociological imagination. Too often we forget about or underplay the "imagination" in the "sociological imagination." Constructing a social study is a creative act involving a particular kind of imagination. Creating a work of art requires artistic imagination; producing a work of fiction, a literary imagination; designing a building, an architectural imagination; constructing a social study, a sociological imagination.

How well does the author of the study you are evaluating use their sociological imagination to transform the topic of their study into a social or intellectual problem? Making that judgment is the second step in evaluating the theorizing that underlies a social study. If you are a little hazy on precisely what we mean by a topic, a social or intellectual problem, and the relationship between the two, you might want to review the section in Chapter 2, "Addressing Social and Intellectual Problems" to refresh your memory.

I compare the process of addressing a social or intellectual problem to creating a picture of social life. The author argues, in effect, that the problem exists because the social world looks and works the way it is depicted in that picture. If the problem being addressed is an intellectual problem connected to a social problem, the author may argue that that the intellectual problem exists because the prevailing conception of the relevant part of the social world suggests it looks and works one way when it actually looks and works another way. In Berger's (1963) terms, "things aren't as they seem." Once the relevant part of the social world is reconceived in the way the author suggests, the problem should be soluble in ways it may not have been before, or so the author argues.

Selection of the Best Concepts, Methods, and Data

The picture of social life the analyst draws is constructed with tools and materials—concepts and data constructed with research methodologies. Evaluating the theorizing that underlies a study involves making a judgment on how well the author of the study has selected his or her tools and materials. Has the author selected the best concepts, the best data, used the best methods to construct her or his picture? Might other concepts or different data constructed with other methods have worked better?

How did Wolf find the data she uses to draw her picture of life for different kinds of women in developed societies? The simple but not inaccurate answer is that she knew where to look. Knowing what to look for and knowing where to find it is key to successfully addressing a problem. Wolf also used creativity and drive. How did she find out what people like her have done with their lives and why they did what they did? She asked her friends. She conducted detailed, open-ended interviews with people she knew. She then used these interviews to illustrate and confirm the quantitative data she found in other sources. You no doubt have different friendship networks than Wolf, but you have networks, and you should feel free to use them when you construct a social study.

Was caste the best concept for Alexander to use to describe the historical condition of African Americans in United States, or would underclass have worked better? Was civic culture the best concept with which to demonstrate widespread consensus amongst Americans in the 1960s? Was crime rate the best measure of honesty in Murray's new lower class? Did Kathryn Edin and Maria Kefalas' study of poor single mothers in one Philadelphia neighborhood provide enough data for Wolf to infer the motives of poor single mothers in the developed world? These are the kinds of questions you need to ask and answer when you evaluate the theorizing in a social study.

How Well Does the Author of Your Study Use Their Tools?

You can't construct a compelling picture of a social reality without the right tools and materials; but even the best tools and materials don't a picture make. The author of a social study has to use the tools, materials, and methods he or she selects with creativity, skill, and imagination. Evaluating the creativity, skill, and imagination the author of a study has demonstrated in the use of their tools, materials, and methods should be a crucial part of the evaluation of the theorizing underlying a social study.

How Well Does the Picture Constructed Depict the Problem Addressed?

The author of a social study uses theoretical concepts, data, and research methods to construct a pattern of connections that constitute a picture of social reality. Wolf, for instance, begins her study with her own life history, and uses the concept of cohort (though not the term) to connect her life experience to that of women of the same generation in situations much like her own. She uses the concept of developed society to connect her cohort with that of similar cohorts of women growing up at the same time in countries like her own. She uses concepts (educational attainment, profession, income, gender, age, marriage, and child-rearing) to connect the experiences of these cohorts of women and to separate these cohorts from other women. Wolf invents the concept of hinge generation to characterize this connection and separation. Their education at elite universities, their jobs, the level of their income from those jobs, their sex lives, the age at which they marry, who (and if) they marry, and their child-rearing practices (if they have children), Wolf argues, separated this hinge generation of women from other women, and in doing so unwittingly contributed to the growing social and economic inequality in developed societies.

The pattern of connections created should depict a part of social reality in a way that reveals the nature of the social and intellectual problem being addressed in the study you are evaluating. Does it accomplish that task? In the end, *Coming Apart* has to be evaluated on the basis of whether or not Murray has constructed a compelling picture of the contemporary United States coming apart. The theorizing in *The New Jim Crow* succeeds to the extent that Alexander is able to paint a convincing picture of the mass incarceration of poor, young, African American men as another form of racialized caste like slavery and Jim Crow segregation.

The XX Factor attempts to construct a portrait of well-educated, upper-middle-class professional women by connecting their high levels of educational attainment, professional lives, income levels, sex lives, marriages, and child-rearing practices into a lifestyle that connects them more to men with similar backgrounds than to other women with different backgrounds. These women, Wolf says, have escaped the gender caste but have increased social inequality in developed societies in the process. Does the picture Wolf paints convincingly make this point? If it does, Wolf's theorizing must be judged a success.

Ultimately, the theorizing you are evaluating must be judged in similar terms. If the author of the study you are examining has successfully painted a picture of social life that convincingly demonstrates the nature of the social or intellectual problem it is designed to address, you must judge it a success; if the picture painted fails to do that, you must show where and why, in your view, it fails.

I would give theorizing that constructs a pattern of social connections that successfully shows why the problem being addressed exists high marks, even if it only provides a sketch of how social life would have to be altered for the problem to be solved. I think that is all that Murray and Alexander provide, and more than Wolf does. I wouldn't judge their theorizing a failure for that reason, though *The XX Factor* might have been a more complete and better study for Wolf if she had.

I think the theorizing in studies like Kovach's *Indigenous Methodologies* has to be evaluated somewhat differently than studies like Murray's, Alexander's, and Wolf's, because her study is trying to do something different and is directed at different audiences. In *Indigenous Methodologies*, Kovach attempts to convey the Indigenous way of thinking to Westerners in terms they can understand, while at the same time making certain that her study is accessible to people in the Indigenous community she is studying. Her study should be evaluated by two different audiences with different criteria of judgment. As a Western academic, I apply one set of criteria; the members of the community she studies apply another. As a result, it is possible for a study like Kovach's to be a success at one level for one audience, and found wanting at another level by another audience.

Once you have judged the problem a study attempts to address as significant, the theorizing that underlies the study has to be evaluated on how successfully it addresses that problem. In the case of Kovach's study, I think you have to begin by examining how well she has selected the concepts she employs in her decolonizing lens. Do they provide a bridge that enables us to cross from the Western way of thinking to the indigenous way of thinking? I think her selection of elements from feminist theorizing and critical theorizing, phenomenology and Marxist theorizing provides such a bridge. However, Kovach's account of Indigenous thinking itself would have been stronger had she provided some examples of the stories that are so central to it. That said, she gave me enough to see how different indigenous thinking is from the thinking that occurs within a paradigm like that in which Murray, Alexander, and Wolf think. Moreover, there seem to me to be aspects of indigenous thought that might well be integrated into Western thinking.

Thinking Well, Living Well, and Being a Good Person

The Indigenous linkage between thinking well, living well, and being a good person is worth emulating, as is the emphasis on maintaining a critical awareness of our studies and our relationship to our studies. Evaluating social studies on the basis of whether they make the communities studied, and the authors and readers of such studies, better also strikes me as worthwhile. Moreover, the objective of "seeking ways to understand the world without harming it" is a good one to pursue. How well does the study you are evaluating meet these criteria?

Kovach's study also needs to be evaluated in the terms the Indigenous communities have themselves set for such studies. The elders in these communities require those who study them and the studies they perform to "do good," and they reserve the right to determine what that good is. Such studies must be accessible to the members of the community studied and evaluated in terms of whether or not the studies create a favorable view of their community in the outside world. These are criteria which only members of the Indigenous communities studied are in a position to apply. When evaluating the theorizing in a study, don't try to do what you aren't in a position to do.

Doing Your Own Theorizing: Constructing a Research Project Proposal

Assume you have the opportunity to spend a semester doing a research project on a topic and problem of your own choosing, and will receive 12 to 15 hours of academic credit for doing so. In order to do the project for credit, however, you first need to write a research project proposal and have it approved by a faculty sponsor. The proposal will describe the theorizing that underlies your project. Your final assignment is to write such a proposal. Below is an outline of the steps to follow in writing your proposal.

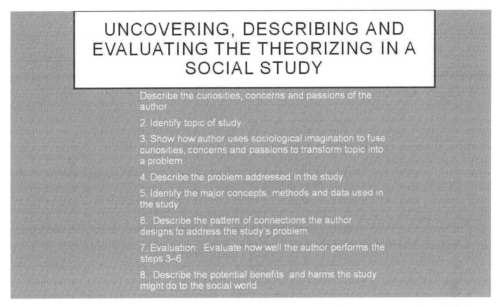

UNCOVERING, DESCRIBING AND EVALUATING THE THEORIZING IN A SOCIAL STUDY

1. Describe the curiosities, concerns and passions of the author

2. Identify topic of study

3. Show how author uses sociological imagination to fuse curiosities, concerns and passions to transform topic into a problem

4. Describe the problem addressed in the study

5. Identify the major concepts, methods and data used in the study

6. Describe the pattern of connections the author designs to address the study's problem

7. Evaluation: Evaluate how well the author performs the steps 3–6.

8. Describe the potential benefits and harms the study might do to the social world.

Figure 13.1: Template for Uncovering, Describing and Analyzing Social Study

Choosing a Topic and Transforming It into a Problem

Human social life constantly presents us with new things to study. Begin theorizing by selecting a topic that is commensurate with your interests, and which is important and significant. Use your sociological imagination to fuse the topic you have selected with your curiosities, concerns, and passions, and transform it into a social or intellectual problem you want to address. See if you can describe your problem and its significance in a paragraph or two.

What Qualifies You to Investigate This Problem?

You may be interested in a particular social or intellectual problem, but interest alone doesn't justify giving you a semester and 12 to 15 academic credits to study it. To get a research proposal approved, you will have to convince people with the power to say no to say yes. Part of doing that involves showing that you know something about the problem already. Here your life experiences can be important, but included in your life experiences should be other research experiences you may have, courses you have taken, and literature on the problem you have read, along with literature you haven't yet read but which you intend to read as part of your project. In a formal project proposal, this usually comes in the form of a literature review. You need to demonstrate that you are aware of and have read some of the studies that have already been done that address the problem you intend to address. You need to make a case that your approach to the problem will be different from those already taken by others.

Formulate a Hypothesis: Make an Educated Guess as to Why the Problem You Want to Address Exists

Brainstorm a bit. Think about the social conditions that have brought about the problem you want to address. Develop a hunch or formulate a textbook version of a hypothesis (an educated guess) on the relationship between these conditions and the problem. See if you can formulate a statement in something like the following form: the problem I want to address exists because the social world looks and works like this. Describe the relationship between these social conditions and the problem as best you can. Don't worry at this point about whether or not you're right. There is plenty of time to think about that later.

Identify the Major Concepts, the Methodological Approach, and the Data You Propose Employing to Do Your Research

Think about what tools and materials you would need to use to show that the social world looks and works in a way that accounts for the problem you want to address. Alternately, think about what tools and materials you would need to show that the world is not as it seems, but actually looks and works very differently. In this second case, you are going to argue something to the effect that if the social world looked and worked the way most people think it does, the problem you are addressing would have been solved long ago.

Describe the major concepts and how you intend to use them. Identify what kinds of data you propose to use and how you will locate or create it. Are you going to conduct interviews? What kind of interviews, and how many? How do you intend to find the people you propose to interview? Are you going to do an ethnographic study? If so, you need to show how you intend to do so. Do you have an informant? How do you propose to convince the people you intend to study to let you study them? If your study is going to rely heavily on existing literature or established data sources, you need to identify the literature and the data sources.

If you intend to employ quantitative databases to address your problem, you need to identify which databases you intend to use, and where they can be located. "On the Internet and in the library" won't cut it here. If you are going to use online databases, you need to give the URLs of the databases and say what you will look for within them. If you are going to use documents and studies in your college's library, you need to identify what they are.

What Might Prove You Wrong?

I think its okay to start with intuitions or gut feelings about why you think the problem you want to address exists, but if you do so you have to be on guard against what is called confirmation bias. Your project has to do more than just search for anything that you can find that indicates that your intuitions and gut feelings are right. To be objective in the sense we have used that term here, you need to identify and search for inconvenient facts and information that would prove your intuitions and gut feelings wrong. You need to describe what facts and information would tend to prove your hunch is off-base. Part of your research would be an active search for such facts and information. In your proposal, you need to state where you intend to look for these facts and this information.

Drawing Your Picture: Designing a Pattern of Connections

To demonstrate that in the early 1960s Americans shared the same culture, Murray established a pattern of connections between different aspects of social life. He provided evidence that most Americans at the time owned the same kinds of cars, watched the same television programs, listened to the same music on the radio, went to the same movies, and believed in and largely practiced the same virtues—religiosity, family, industriousness, and honesty.

To demonstrate that contemporary upper-middle-class professional women had escaped the gender caste and had unwittingly increased social inequality in the process, Wolf tried to establish a pattern of connections between aspects of social life these women shared, but which increasingly separated them from other women. Their education, jobs, incomes, sex lives, leisure activities, husbands, and child-rearing practices united these 20 percent of women in developed societies and increasingly separated them from the other 80 percent of women, who by and large remained within the gender caste.

To address the social problem you propose, you need to identify the aspects of social life you intend to connect and identify as precisely as you can, and describe what you think this pattern of connections demonstrates. In our terms, you need to show how the way the social world looks and works explains why the social problem

Research Project Proposal

1. Curiosities, Concerns, and Passions
2. Topic
3. Problem and Hypothesis
4. Qualifications
5. Basic Concepts, Methodological Approach, and data
6. Inconvenient facts: describe and identify where you would search for them
7. Patterns of Connections
8. Making you and the people you study better

Figure 13.2: Template for Research Project Proposal

you intend to address exists. If you think you can also demonstrate or at least suggest how the world would have to look and work differently for your problem to be solved, you should certainly say so.

MAKING YOURSELF, THE PEOPLE YOU STUDY, AND THE SOCIAL WORLD BETTER

Your project proposal should show how it will make you and the people you intend to study better, and the world a better place in which to live. I'm not suggesting that you demonstrate that you are in possession of divine powers. You just need to show that the project you propose meets the ethical strictures of research on Indigenous communities outlined by Kovach. Maintain critical awareness of what you intended to study and your relationship to it. What do you think you will gain by doing your project? Will your project serve the people you propose to study? Will your project help you understand the world without harming it?

ASSIGNMENTS

1. Use your answers to the study questions and relevant assignments in previous chapters to construct an outline of an essay that uncovers, describes, and evaluates the theorizing that underlies the reading(s) you have chosen to analyze.

2. Use the outline you have constructed to write an essay uncovering, describing, and evaluating the theorizing that underlies the readings you have chosen to examine.

CHAPTER 14

SOCIAL THEORIZING AND SOCIAL CHANGE

"Here I stand; I can do no other. God help me."
Martin Luther, Diet of Worms

*"There is no way in which any social scientist can avoid assuming choices of
value and implying them in his work as a whole. Problems, like issues and
troubles, concern threats to expected values, and cannot be clearly formulated
without acknowledgment of those values."*
C. Wright Mills, *The Sociological Imagination*

*"It is true to say, provided it is rightly understood, that successful politics is
always 'the art of the possible'. It is no less true, however, that the possible
is very often achieved only by reaching out towards the impossible
which lies beyond it."*
Max Weber, "Value-judgments in Social Science"

*"Philosophers have hitherto only interpreted the world in various ways; the
point is to change it."*
Karl Marx, Theses on Feuerbach

THE ROLE OF THEORIZING IN PROMOTING SOCIAL CHANGE

Recent studies and my own teaching experience indicate that many of you decided to major in a social science because you want to promote positive social change and better understand your position in society (Spalter-Roth and Van Vourer 2009; American Sociological Association 2012). One of the knocks on social theory is that it doesn't help people promote necessary social change. Many of you, like Marx, don't just want to understand society; you want to change it. I want to conclude this book by making the case for the importance of theorizing in promoting social change.

The theorizing we have discussed here can and has played a major role in promoting social change. If you want to make changes to the social world you have to first

Figure 14.1: Change the World

understand it. If you want to try to solve social problems and promote social justice, you should have a clear idea why the problems you address, and the injustices you want to redress, exist. Theorizing is a necessary part of addressing social problems and social injustices. When you theorize, you in effect say that the problems and injustices you want to address exist because the social world looks and works the way you say it does. For problems to be solved and injustices redressed, the social world has to look and work differently than it does now. In other words, you have to construct both an explanation of what about the existing world causes social problems and social injustices to exist, and an argument for how those causes might be removed.

VALUES AND SOCIAL CHANGE

Values play a critical role in promoting social change, as they do in social theorizing. Social values involve judgments of condemnation or approval of social actions. Social values also provide motives for social actions. Every choice between alternative possible social actions involves, explicitly or implicitly, consciously or unconsciously, a value judgment. It is a decision as to what we "ought" to do, given our stance toward the social world in which we live. When we theorize about social life, we don't do so from a position above it, observing what goes on below. We don't just study or theorize about social life, we also live it. "No one is 'outside society'; the question is where each stands within it" (Mills 1959, 184).

To work and act in a socially conscious way, we must locate ourselves within the intellectual and social life of our times. Key to establishing that location is the development of a perspective, a stance toward the world in which we live. This stance is inevitably based on value judgments. Max Weber argued, I think correctly, that while values are intertwined and entangled with virtually every attitude which we adopt, science cannot provide a basis for such judgments (Weber, 1946, 69). We shouldn't look to science to make these judgments for us. Value judgments are matters of morality, not science.

DEVELOPING A PERSPECTIVE AND TAKING A STANCE

In 1521, Martin Luther was summoned to appear before a tribunal convened by Emperor Charles V and asked to renounce the "heretical" views contained in his writings and sermons. "Asked" is probably not the right term. To be accused of heresy in sixteenth-century Europe was serious business. To refuse to renounce views that had been judged heretical might well cost you your life. Luther refused to retract his views and instead defended them at some length. The key works he was being asked to renounce, he argued, attacked the abuses of the Christian world and could not be renounced without encouraging those abuses to continue. According to tradition, Luther concluded his defense by saying, "I cannot and will not recant anything, since it is neither safe nor right to go against conscience. Here I stand. I can do no other. May God help me" (Luther 1904). While scholars debate whether these were Luther's exact words, there is no dispute about Luther's position. Through his writings and sermons, his theorizing, he had taken a position within the intellectual and social life of his time. His stance toward the world in which he lived was a moral one, one from which he refused to back away.

The intellectual and social life of our time is very different from Luther's. However, placing oneself within it, developing a perspective with which to view it, and taking a stance toward it remain matters of morality or, in our terms, value judgments. This is true both of those we generally classify as conservative thinkers and those we classify as liberal or radical thinkers. Thinkers who view the world from different perspectives give a different answer to the ancient Greek questions of how we should live and how we should live together.

CHARLES MURRAY'S STANCE

Charles Murray frames his stance toward our world in terms of two alternative conceptions of the good life. Murray characterizes (unfairly in my view) one of these conceptions as the "European Syndrome":

> The purpose of life is to while away the time between birth and death as pleasantly as possible, and the purpose of government is to make it as easy as possible to while away the time as pleasantly as possible. (Murray 2012, 284)

He contrasts this European Syndrome with what he calls the "American Project":

> The alternative to the European Syndrome is to say that your life can have transcendent meaning if it is spent doing important things—raising a family, supporting yourself, being a good friend and a good neighbor, learning what you can do well and then doing it as well as you possibly can. Providing the best possible framework for doing those things is what the American Project is all about. (Murray 2012, 284)

I would fault Murray's characterization of these alternatives (the first is more caricature than characterization; the second more panegyric than description), but not his attempt to situate himself within the intellectual and social life of his time, and not for taking a stance toward it. The theorizing he does in *Coming Apart* is based upon this value judgment, his moral choice between the alternative conceptions of life he calls the European Syndrome and the American Project.

MICHELLE ALEXANDER'S STANCE

Michelle Alexander conceives of the social and intellectual life of our time in very different terms than does Murray. She also takes a different stance toward it. Alexander sees American history in terms of the conflict amongst classes and ethnic and racial groups. When rich whites have succeeded in using racism to divide poor white, ethnic, and racial groups against each other, she argues, they have succeeded in maintaining their position at the top of a combined class- and caste-based system.

When poor white, ethnic, and racial groups have united against wealthy elites, they have, Alexander argues, successfully challenged that system, for a time. In response to this challenge, wealthy elites have changed the form of the system in order to maintain their dominant position in it. "Segregation had afforded elites a crucial means of exercising control over poor and working class whites as well as blacks. The Southern white elite, whether planters or industrialists, had successfully endeavored to make all whites think in racial rather than class terms, predictably leading whites to experience desegregation ... as net 'loss'" (Alexander 2012, 257).

Alexander takes a clear stance toward the intellectual and social life of her time as she conceives it. She sides with the poor white, ethnic, and racial groups against wealthy elites. She chooses to celebrate racial and ethnic differences rather than call for a post-racial society. "We should hope not for a colorblind society but instead for a world in which we can see each other fully, learn from each other, and do what we can to respond to each other with love" (244). Alexander favors a society "in which all human beings of all races are treated with dignity and have the right to food, shelter, health care, education and security" (259). This is Alexander's answer to the ancient Greek question of how we should live and how we should live together. Her answer is as much a value judgment and a moral stance as was Luther's and Murray's. It is central to her study, *The New Jim Crow*.

CAPITAL IN THE TWENTY-FIRST CENTURY: THOMAS PIKETTY'S STANCE

Thomas Piketty's *Capital in the Twenty-First Century* (2014) is a detailed historical study of economic growth in developed countries. Based on analysis of a great deal of new data, Piketty brings into question the orthodox position on income inequality in developed countries. According to the orthodox position, usually referred to as the Kuznets curve, income inequality is greatest at the beginning of the development process and progressively lessens as the development process matures. Piketty's theoretical interpretation of the new data he has assembled indicates that, historically, income inequality in developed countries has instead taken a U-shape. Income inequality is great at the beginning of the development process, lessens in the middle, and is great again as developed countries reach a mature phase of slower growth.

> This "U shaped curve" reflects an absolutely crucial transformation ... the return of high capital/income ratios over the past few decades can be explained in large part by the return to a regime of slow growth. ... If, moreover, the return on capital remains significantly above the growth rate for an extended period of time (which is more likely when the growth

rate is low, though not automatic) th[e]n the risk of divergence in the distribution of wealth is very high. (Piketty 2014, 25).

While *Capital in the Twenty-First Century* has been wildly successful, topping the Amazon bestseller list for many weeks and selling out quickly after it appeared in English, its importance for the discussion here lies in what it is not and what it does not purport to be. Piketty's argument is not one of economic determinism. He does not make an interpretation of future happenings based on an economic model. Instead, Piketty argues that income distribution is more a matter of values and political struggle than of automatic economic market mechanisms.

"The history of inequality is shaped by the way economic, social and political actors view what is just and what is not, as well as the relative power of those actors and the collective choices that result" (Piketty 2014, 20). In the end, Piketty argues, income inequality is shaped more by the values of social actors than market forces. People's conception of what is just and fair, what groups with which values manage to work their will over others, ultimately determines whether economic inequality increases or is lessened.

The Use of Reason in the Furtherance of Values

Social theorizing is at least in part the use of reason in the furtherance of values. It has the potential to expand the realm of human freedom by identifying the possibilities and consequences of human action. While I don't think social theorizing can identify the correct moral position toward the world, the right value judgments to make on it, or the ethically correct actions to take within it, I do think it can broaden our understanding of our world, and enable us to understand different possible ways to situate ourselves within it and different perspectives that can be taken toward it. Theorizing can broaden the context of reflection within which we make our moral choices and better enable us to think through the consequences of the actions we take in defense of the values we choose.

Theorizing and Promoting Social Change

Social theorizing can be conceived of as the construction of a picture of social life, what it looks like, and how it works, and the connection of that picture to the problem the theorizing is designed to address. Optimally, theorizing should also include an account of how that picture would have to be altered for the problem being addressed to be successfully solved. Theorizing about social change requires an additional element. It should take the form of an account of the various means through which the way things are can be transformed into the way things would need to be for the problem addressed to be solved.

Theorizing about social change should provide an evaluation of the possibility of making the kind of transformation that would be involved in solving the problem being addressed. If there is no realistic possibility of making the required transformation by any viable means, those theorizing social change should say so and explain why. If the transformation necessary to solve the problem being addressed is feasible, those doing the theorizing should identify and describe the alternative means that might be employed to make this transformation. The description of each of those means should include an evaluation of its likelihood of success and the likely consequences of its failure.

Those theorizing about social change should also include an account of the likely side effects of employing each of the alternative means available. It may well be that these side effects contradict the very values the solution to the problem being addressed is designed to further. By identifying these factors, theorizing can provide a context within which informed decisions on how to change social life in the furtherance of social values can be made and what the likely costs of that change will probably entail.

To Whom Do We Wish to Direct Our Theorizing?

When we theorize, we should not only be mindful of the position we occupy in the intellectual life and social structure of our time and the values we wish to further, we should also identify the audience to whom we want to direct our theorizing. It is possible to direct our theorizing at elites who have the power to implement the changes we want, and know it; or, we can direct our theorizing at those who may have such power but are unaware of it; or at those without power whose awareness of social life is confined to their everyday milieu but who, exposed to good theorizing and equipped with a sociological imagination, might actively attempt to change the social conditions within which they find themselves (Mills 1959, 185).

Theorizing about social change, even if it is directed at actors in a position to implement change, doesn't in itself produce change. It can, however, provide inspiration and guidance to people who can. Charles Murray didn't alter social welfare policy in the United States. His books, *Losing Ground* (1984) and *The Bell Curve* (1994), did, however, have an impact on the people who did. Michelle Alexander didn't change drug policy in the United States, nor did she make the decisions that altered sentencing guidelines for people convicted of possession of crack cocaine. Her book, *The New Jim Crow*, however, clearly influenced the people who did try to make those decisions and changes. Thomas Piketty hasn't reduced economic inequality in the contemporary world, but his book, *Capital in the Twenty-First Century*, may offer encouragement and guidance to people who might attempt to do so.

Theorizing and Doing Social Change

Those who follow Marx's suggestion and opt to change the world rather than only interpret it should understand that well-crafted and carefully conceived interpretations of the world can be helpful tools in changing it.

In the contemporary world, people who wish to dedicate themselves to social change and the promotion of social justice are often contemptuous of politics. They conceive of "politics" as working for a major political party, running for office, or campaigning for those who do. People who want to promote social change in a way that advances social justice often condemn the major political parties in the nation states in which they live as impotent or corrupt. To the extent that political parties have become little more than large-scale organizations designed to win elections, control political offices, and secure positions in the political bureaucracy for their members, it is not surprising that those interested in social justice and social change condemn them.

Theorizing and Social Movements

Those who decide to advance the cause of social justice by participating in social movements have thereby decided to use political power to achieve their objectives. In Max Weber's terms, they have chosen politics as a vocation (Weber, 1965, 212–26). The decision to participate in or help form parties, movements, and publics within which ideas and alternatives of social life are truly debated, and which have a chance to play a role in the decisions of structural consequence (Mills 1959, 190), is the decision to try to make history. C. Wright Mills was correct when he said that "if men [women] do not make history, they tend increasingly to become the utensils of history-makers and also the mere objects of history-making" (Mills 1959, 181). That said, "laying one's hands on the spokes of the wheels of history" (Weber, 1965, 212) involves particular hazards, satisfactions, frustrations, and ethical dilemmas. Real politics is not for the faint of heart or the weak of mind. Those who commit themselves to real politics in this sense should understand what such a decision entails.

Power and the Advancement of Social Justice

The decision to participate in real politics involves harnessing and directing one's passion toward the advancement of a realistic cause. The advancement of that cause necessitates viewing things and people as they really are, not as one might wish they were or would like them to be. Participation in real politics involves the use of power. Power is the major tool necessary to promote social justice and advance social change.

The use of power should be accompanied by a conscious awareness of the irrationality of some aspects of the social world and the consequent limitation of efforts to transform this irrationality, with reason. The inevitable limitations of such efforts can lead to frustration and disillusionment. Such frustration and disillusionment often leads to using power for self-aggrandizement and enrichment (Weber, 1965, 214). The corruption of the political process, like the road to hell, is often paved with good intentions.

Ethics and the Use of Power to Further Social Change

Max Weber was strongly opposed to professors using their classrooms as platforms from which to advance their political positions. To advocate particular political positions to an audience of largely silent students whose future careers could be influenced by the evaluations of their professors was, in his view, an abuse of the position. Weber was not opposed to professors' involvement in politics. He himself was actively involved in the politics of his time (see Mommsen 1984). What he opposed was professors using the classroom to advance their politics.

In 1918, Weber gave a lecture titled "Politics as a Vocation" (Weber [1919] 1965) to a largely student audience, at their invitation. His audience included a large number of young people who were contemptuous of the old order and anxious to involve themselves in radical movements of social change. Weber's lecture was not an attempt to discourage German youth from participation in movements of social change. He instead urged those who did so to understand what serious political commitment involved, and what those who made such a commitment should be prepared to expect. One hundred years later, much of what Weber said remains relevant to those who contemplate committing themselves to participation in movements dedicated to social justice and social change.

THE ETHICS OF INTENTION

Central to Weber's comments was the distinction between what he called "the ethics of intention" and "the ethics of responsibility." No one has the right to tell another which ethic to follow. However, Weber cautions, ethics should not be viewed as "a cab which one can hail at will, to get in or out as one sees fit" (Weber, 1965, 216). Those who choose to follow the ethics of intention commit themselves to doing what is good and moral as they see it, regardless of the consequences. When we employ the ethics of intention we act rightly and leave the outcome to God, the gods, or to fate. The ethics of intention can motivate acts of protest against injustice; but such acts are expressions, not tactics in a strategy designed to promote social justice. I have engaged in many a protest against what I perceived to be social injustices with no expectation that my protest would have any effect other than to express my opposition. In this sense my protests were not really political acts. The ethics of intention can never justify bad actions in an effort to advance good causes. According to the ethics of intention, good actions are taken because they are good, regardless of their effect.

THE ETHICS OF RESPONSIBILITY

Movements for social justice and social change, to have any chance of success, must follow an ethic of responsibility, not intention. According to this ethic, actions are taken precisely because of their intended effect, for the advancement of a cause. Such actions involve the use of power to effect change. It is simply not true, Weber argues, that only good comes from good actions and only bad from bad actions. "Not only the whole course of human history, but every incontrovertible test of everyday experience makes it plain the opposite is true" (Weber, 1965, 219). Those who want to participate in social movements to advance social justice should be prepared to use ethically dubious means to do so and be prepared to take responsibility for their actions. Sometimes the ends do justify the means; sometimes they don't. Deciding which is the case in any particular situation is the kind of ethical judgment people have to make frequently when they follow the ethics of responsibility.

Movements for social justice attract a variety of people with a variety of motives. Some people join because they are lonely and want to meet people; some people join because they are angry or resentful and want an outlet for their anger or resentment. Some people join movements to list their participation as a form of community service on their résumés. It is wise to be aware of the motives of those who are part of the movement one participates in, and, for that matter, to be constantly aware of one's own motives. However, any movement that only accepts good people with pure motives as members will be small and probably ineffective (Weber, 1965, 222).

Movements for social justice rarely, if ever, accomplish their ends completely. Even the most successful movements achieve only partial victories. Almost always, even these limited successes are accompanied by less than desirable side effects. Those who commit themselves to an ethic of responsibility and all those who devote themselves to the advancement of social justice in this world must judge their actions on the basis of whether or not the good they accomplish outweighs the bad they tolerate or even participate in to accomplish it.

Even by these standards, movements for social justice often fail. Those who wish to devote their energy to such movements "must arm themselves with that stoutness of heart which is able to confront even the shipwreck of all their hopes. ... Only someone who is confident [she] he will not be shattered if the world, seen from his [her] point of view is too stupid or too vulgar for what [she] he wants to offer it; someone who can say, in spite of that 'but still' ... has a vocation for politics" (Weber, 1965, 225).

CONCLUSION

I hope I have been able to persuade you that social theory can be more than a course you are required to take, another hoop you must jump through to get your degree. It can be more than simply a struggle to comprehend the works of famous theorists whose eloquence and complexity make them difficult to understand, let alone evaluate and put to any practical use. It should be said that this is not the way these theorists themselves viewed their work. Marx, Weber, Durkheim, Foucault, and Habermas were very much involved in the social life and politics of their time, and hoped that their writings would contribute to changing the world for the better. I think all thoughtful students of social life feel this way.

If we look at a theory as an attempt to explain an aspect of social life, and theorizing as the attempt to construct such an explanation, then every thoughtful study of social life is a work of theory constructed through theorizing. I have tried to demonstrate that by uncovering, describing, and evaluating studies written by contemporary authors on issues of social import to our time. I offer my analysis of these works as examples of how to uncover, describe, and evaluate the theorizing that underlies thoughtful social studies. My objective in doing so is to help you to uncover, describe, and analyze studies on your own. I think the process of analyzing the theorizing that underlies all thoughtful studies of social life is an important skill to develop, not just for those of you who want to be social scientists, but for all of you who want to better understand your position in social life and want to change the societies in which you live for the better.

Learning how to analyze the theorizing of others is an important step to learning how to theorize yourself. To learn to theorize is to learn how to construct explanations of aspects of social life about which you are curious, to address social problems about which you are concerned, and redress forms of social injustice about which you are passionate. If you want to understand your position in the social life of which you are a part, or try to change the society in which live, you have to understand how it works. Theorizing is part of the effort to gain that understanding.

Assignment

1. Reread your first essay and your notes on the end-of-chapter assignments on producing a research project proposal. Following the template provided at the end of Chapter 12, construct a research project proposal.

Suggested Further Readings

Weber, Max. [1919] 1965. *Politics as a Vocation*. Philadelphia: Fortress Press.

Weber, Max. [1919] 1946. "Science as Vocation." From *Max Weber*, Edited and Translated by Hans Gerth and C. Wright Mills. New York: Free Press.

Image Credit

Fig. 14.1: Copyright © by Depositphotos / gustavofrazao.

BIBLIOGRAPHY

Alexander, Michelle. 2012. *The New Jim Crow: Mass Incarceration in the Age of Colorblindness*, rev. ed. New York: The New Press.

American Sociological Association. 2012. *Bachelor's and Beyond Survey.*

ASA.theory.org/theory-syllabi.htm

Babbie, Earl. 2010. *The Practice of Social Research*. Belmont, CA: Wadsworth.

Basirico, Lawrence A., Barbara G. Cashion, and J. Ross Eshleman. 2014. *Introduction to Sociology*. Redding, CA: BVT Publishing.

Baxandall, Michael. 1985. *Patterns of Intention*. New Haven, CT: Yale University Press.

Berger, Peter L. 1963. *An Invitation to Sociology*. Garden City, NY: Doubleday Anchor Books.

Black, Sandra E., and Chinhui Juhn. "The Rise of Female Professionals: Are Women Responding to Skill Demand?" *American Economic Review*, 90 (2): 450–455.

Bourdieu, Pierre.1984. *Distinction: A Social Critique of the Judgement of Taste*. Translated by Richard Nice. Cambridge: Harvard University Press.

Brooks, David. 2000. *Bobos in Paradise*. New York: Simon and Schuster.

Brown, Susan L. 2004. "Family Structure and Child Well-Being: The Significance of Parental Cohabitation." *Journal of Marriage and the Family* 66 (May): 351–67.

Brown, Susan L. 2006. Family Structures Transitions and Adolescent Well Being. *Demography* 43 (3): 447–61.

Cole, David. 1999. *No Equal Justice: Race and Class in the American Criminal Justice System.* New York: The New Press.

Cox, Oliver. 1959. *Caste, Class and Race.* New York: Monthly Review Press.

Danto, Arthur D. 1965. *Analytical Philosophy of History.* Cambridge: Cambridge University Press.

Dollard, John. 1949. *Class, Caste and Race in a Southern Town.* Madison: University of Wisconsin Press.

Dunlop, C. 2009. "Female Power." *The Economist*, December 30.

Durkheim, Emile. [1938] 1965. *The Rules of Sociological Method*, 8th ed. Translated by Sarah A. Solavay and John H. Mueller. Edited by George E.G. Catlin. New York: Free Press.

———. [1938] 1951. *Suicide: A Study of Sociology.* Translated by John A. Spaulding and George Simpson. Edited by George Simpson. New York: Free Press.

Edin, Kathryn, and Maria Kefalas. 2005. *Promises I Can Keep: Why Poor Women Put Motherhood before Marriage.* Berkeley: University of California Press.

Foucault, Michel. 1965. *Madness and Civilization.* Translated by Richard Howard. New York: New American Library.

Fresia, Gerald. 1998. *Toward an American Revolution: Exposing the Constitution and Other Illusions.* Boston: South End Press.

Geiger, Roger. 2002. *The Future of the City of Intellect*, edited by Steven Brint. Palo Alto, CA: Stanford University Press.

Gersbuny, Jonathan, and Oriel Sullivan. 1998. "The Sociological Uses of Time-Use Diary Analysis." *European Sociological Review* 14 (1): 69–85.

Giddens, Anthony. 1984. *The Constitution of Society*. Berkeley and Los Angeles: University of California Press.

Giddens, Anthony, Mitchell Duneier, Richard P. Applebaum, and Deborah Carr. 2013. *Essentials of Sociology*. New York: Norton.

Goffman, Irving. 1959. *The Presentation of Self in Everyday Life*. New York: Anchor Books.

Goldin, Claudia, and Robert A. Margo. 1991. *The Great Compression: The Wage Structure in the United States at Mid-Century*. Working Paper No. 3817. NBER Working Paper Series. Cambridge, MA: National Bureau of Economic Research.

Gould, Kenneth A., and Tammy L. Lewis. 2014. *Ten Lessons in Introductory Sociology*. New York: Oxford University Press.

Graham, Mary. 2008. "Some Thoughts about the Philosophical Underpinnings of Aboriginal Wordviews." *Australian Humanities Review* 45 (November). http://www.australianhumanitiesreview.org/archive/Issue-November-2008/graham.html

Habermas, Jürgen. 1996. *On the Logic of the Social Sciences*. Boston: Massachusetts Institute of Technology Press.

Haig-Brown, Celia. 2008. "Taking Indigenous Thought Seriously: A Rant on Globalization with Some Cautionary Notes." *Journal of the Canadian Association of Curriculum Studies*. Toronto: York University. http://jcacs.journals.yorku.ca/index.php/jcacs/article/viewFile/17997/16859.

Hakim, Catherine. 2011. *Honey Money: The Power of Erotic Capital*. London: Allen Lane.

Hochschild, Arlie. 2016. "I Spent 5 Years with Some of Trump's Biggest Fans. Here's What They Won't Tell You." *Mother Jones*, September/October.

Herrnstein, Richard J., and Charles Murray. 1994. *The Bell Curve*. New York: The Free Press.

Kovach, Margaret. 2009. *Indigenous Methodologies: Characteristics, Conversations, and Contexts.* Toronto: University of Toronto Press.

Kuhn, Thomas S. 1962. *The Structure of Scientific Revolutions.* Chicago: University of Chicago Press.

———. 1989. "The Natural and the Human Sciences." In *The Road Since Structure, 216–224,* edited by James Conant and John Haugeland. Chicago: University of Chicago Press.

Luther, Martin. 1904. *The Life of Luther Written by Himself,* collected and arranged by M. Michelet. Translated by William Hazlitt. London: George Bell and Sons.

Mannheim, Karl. 1926. "The Ideological and Sociological Interpretation of Phenomena." *From Karl Mannheim,* edited by Kurt Wolff, 116–32. 1971. New York: Oxford University Press.

Margo, Robert A., and Lynne L. 1997. NBER Working Papers 18752. National Bureau of Economic Research, Inc.

Marx, Karl. [1845] 1969. "Theses on Feuerbach." In *Marx/Engels Selected Works,* vol. I, 13–15. Moscow: Progress Publishers.

———. 1859 [1970]. *A Contribution to the Critique of Political Economy.* New York: International Publishers.

Merton, Robert K. 1936. "The Unanticipated Consequences of Purposive Social Action." *American Sociological Review* 1 (6): 895.

Michels, Robert. 1915. *Political Parties.* Glencoe, IL: The Free Press.

Mills, C. Wright. 1959. *The Sociological Imagination.* New York: Oxford University Press.

Mommsen, Wolfgang. 1984. *Max Weber and German Politics 1890–1920.* Translated by Michael S. Steinberg. Chicago: University of Chicago Press.

Morgan, Edmond. 1975. *American Slavery, American Freedom: The Ordeal of Colonial Virginia.* New York: Norton.

Murray, Charles. 1984. *Losing Ground*. New York: Basic Books.

———. 2012. *Coming Apart: The State of White America, 1960–2010*. New York: Crown Publishing.

Obach, Brian. 2014. "Class and Intersectionality." In *Ten Lessons in Introductory Sociology*, edited by Kenneth A. Gould and Tammy Lewis, 151-187, New York: Oxford University Press.

Phillips, Kevin P. 1969. *The Emerging Republican Majority*. Garden City, NY: Doubleday and Company.

Piketty, Thomas. 2014. *Capital in the Twenty-First Century*. Translated by Arthur Goldhammer. Cambridge, MA: Harvard University Press.

Popper, Karl. 1957. *The Poverty of Historicism*. Boston and New York: Routledge.

———. 1976. "The Logic of the Social Sciences." In *The Positivist Dispute in German Sociology*, edited by Theodor Adorno et al. New York: Harper and Row.

Putnam, Robert D. 2000. *Bowling Alone*. New York: Simon and Schuster.

———. 2015. *Our Kids*. New York: Simon and Schuster.

Radkau, Joakhim. 2011. *Max Weber: A Biography*. Translated by Patrick Camiller. Malden, MA: Polity Press.

Ritzer, George. 2015. *Introduction to Sociology*. Thousand Oaks, CA: Sage Publications.

Rosanvallon, Pierre. 2007. "Intellectual History and Democracy: An Interview with Pierre Rosanvallon." *Journal of the History of Ideas* 68, 703–715.

Skocpol, Theda. 2003. *Diminished Democracy*. Norman, OK: University of Oklahoma Press.

Soares, Joseph. 2007. *The Power of Privilege: Yale and America's Elite Colleges*. Palo Alto, CA: Stanford University Press.

Spalter-Roth, Roberta, and Nicole Van Vourer. 2009. "Idealists and Careerists: Graduate Choices for Sociology Majors." *American Sociological Association Department of Research and Development.*

Stamp, Kenneth M. 1965. *The Era of Reconstruction: 1865–1877.* New York: Random House.

Swedberg, Richard. 2014. *The Art of Social Theory.* Princeton, NJ: Princeton University Press.

Swedberg, Richard, ed. 2014. *Theorizing in Social Science.* Palo Alto, CA: Stanford University Press.

Swatos, William H., and Lutz Kaelber, eds. 2005. *The Protestant Ethic Turns 100.* Boulder, CO: Paradigm Publishers.

Tavory, Idoo, and Stefan Timmermans. 2014. *Abductive Analysis: Theorizing Qualitative Research.* Chicago: University of Chicago Press.

Thomas, William, and Dorothy Thomas. 1929. *The Child in America.* New York: Alfred Knopf.

Vance, J. D. 2016. *Hillbilly Elegy.* New York: HarperCollins.

Weaver, Warren J. 1969. "The Emerging Republican Majority." *The New York Times,* September 21, BR3. ProQuest Historical Newspapers.

Weber, Max. 1964. *The Theory of Social and Economic Organization*, edited by Talcott Parsons. New York: The Free Press.

———. [1920] 1972. "Prefatory Remarks to Collected Essays in the Sociology of Religion." The Protestant Ethic and the Spirit of Capitalism with Other Writings on the Rise of the West. 2009. Translated and Introduced by Stephen Kalberg. New York: Oxford University Press, 205–221.

———. 1978. *Economy and Society*, Volume One, edited by Guenther Roth and Claus Wittich. Berkeley: University of California Press.

———. 1965. *Politics as a Vocation.* Philadelphia: Fortress Press.

————. [1919] 1946. "Science as Vocation." From *Max Weber*, Translated and Edited By Hans Gerth and C. Wright Mills. New York: Free Press.

Winch, Peter. 1958. *The Idea of a Social Science*. London: Routledge.

Wolf, Alison. 2013. *The XX Factor: How the Rise of Working Women Has Created a Far Less Equal World*. New York: Crown Publishers.

Woodward, C. Vann. 1955. *The Strange Career of Jim Crow*. New York: Oxford University Press.

INDEX